Kickstart
How Successful Canadians Got Started

Kickstart
How Successful Canadians Got Started

Alexander Herman • Paul Matthews • Andrew Feindel

THE DUNDURN GROUP
TORONTO

Editor: Barry Jowett
Copy-editor: Jennifer Gallant
Designer: Erin Mallory
Printer: Webcom

Library and Archives Canada Cataloguing in Publication

Herman, Alex, 1981-
    Kickstart : how successful Canadians got started / Alex Herman, Paul Matthews, Andrew Feindel.

ISBN 978-1-55002-783-9

    1. Successful people--Canada--Biography. I. Matthews, Paul, 1981-
II. Feindel, Andrew, 1981- III. Title.

FC25.H47 2008   920.071   C2007-907081-7

1 2 3 4 5   13 12 11 10 09 08

Conseil des Arts
du Canada

Canada Council
for the Arts

ONTARIO ARTS COUNCIL
CONSEIL DES ARTS DE L'ONTARIO

Canada

We acknowledge the support of the **Canada Council for the Arts** and the **Ontario Arts Council** for our publishing program. We also acknowledge the financial support of the **Government of Canada** through the **Book Publishing Industry Development Program** and **The Association for the Export of Canadian Books**, and the **Government of Ontario** through the **Ontario Book Publishers Tax Credit program** and the **Ontario Media Development Corporation**.

Care has been taken to trace the ownership of copyright material used in this book. The author and the publisher welcome any information enabling them to rectify any references or credits in subsequent editions.

J. Kirk Howard, President

Printed and bound in Canada
www.dundurn.com

Dundurn Press
3 Church Street, Suite 500
Toronto, Ontario, Canada
M5E 1M2

Gazelle Book Services Limited
White Cross Mills
High Town, Lancaster, England
LA1 4XS

Dundurn Press
2250 Military Road
Tonawanda, NY
U.S.A. 14150

To Our Parents

CONTENTS

SURVIVORS: CANADIANS WHO PERSEVERED

DREAMERS: CANADIANS WHO BLAZED THEIR OWN TRAILS

ACKNOWLEDGEMENTS

We are extremely grateful to all who brought the project to life: Birnie Benton for his inspiration; Susan Feindel and those who helped at Forest Hill Tutoring; Zoë Pope for her enthusiasm; Gary Ross for his advice; Krista Stout, Nicole Monardo, Sharon Franks, and Kate Lunau for their opinions; Alan Sullivan for hosting our "retreat"; John Godfrey for building bridges; Robin De Bled for his web designs; Andy Bull; Adrienne Guthrie; Richard Heller; Dave Barber; Jason McBride; Olivier Plessis; Charles Kassardjian; Vincent Lam; Léonid Sirota; Bill Feindel; Julie Vanderherberg; Marc Weiner; the supportive team at Dundurn; the countless assistants who fit us into busy schedules; and, of course, all those who were interviewed as part of this book — thank you for putting up with us, providing us with and allowing us to use your photographs, and giving us your input on the many revisions.

We would also like to acknowledge CanLyme for its continued battle against Lyme disease in Canada. A portion of the proceeds of this book will be donated to finance research for the many Canadians who need help to combat this disease.

The authors will be donating a portion of the proceeds of this publication to the Canadian Lyme Disease Foundation (CanLyme).

CanLyme
CANADIAN LYME DISEASE
FOUNDATION
FONDATION CANADIENNE
DE LA MALADIE DE LYME

The Canadian Lyme Disease Foundation (CanLyme) exists to enhance awareness, promote education, and fund research into this devastating disease. Lyme disease (LD) is a zoonotic disease, passed from animals to humans. Ticks, mosquitoes, and other biting insects harbour and transmit LD. Mother to fetus transmission was discovered in 1985.

Diseases with no known cause total 1.5 million in Canada. LD has been implicated in many of those, such as multiple sclerosis and other neurological disorders, colitis, Crohn's disease, Alzheimer's disease, irritable bowel syndrome, arthritis, heart and hormonal disorders, autistic-like behaviours, psychiatric disorders, Parkinsonism, chronic fatigue syndrome, fibromyalgia, and hearing and eyesight conditions. Collectively these diseases are bankrupting health care budgets. Testing for LD is woefully inadequate. Canada confirms fewer than sixty cases of LD annually, but we just happen to have some of the highest rates in the world of the aforementioned diseases. Only aggressive post-mortem and live tissue studies will reveal the true extent of LD.

CanLyme recently lost one of its prominent board members, Dr. Satyen Banerjee. He was a pioneer of LD research in Canada while at the British Columbia Centre for Disease Control. His attempt to sound alarms in 1993 in the BC Medical Journal fell on deaf ears. CanLyme will continue to sound the alarm for Dr. Banerjee.

A principle CanLyme goal is to build an LD research facility to do the work that needs to be done. Learn more about LD at www.CanLyme.org.

Jim M. Wilson
President

INTRODUCTION
The Origin of *Kickstart*

It seems so long ago now. We had all just finished university and moved back in with our parents. Mere months since our first exposure to the "real world," we met one evening to lick each other's early employment wounds.

Time magazine had recently labelled ours the "Twixter generation," a cohort who refused to grow up, move out of parental basements, and get down to the serious business of being respectable, child-rearing, and middle class. The supposed "quarter-life crisis" seemed more like clever PR-speak to the three of us, but it was impossible to deny that our friends were more like Hamlet than Howard Hughes. Plagued with questions and devoid of answers, our twenties were not turning out to be the wonderland we'd been promised.

Paul and Alex wanted to be writers — or at least that's what they told fashionable girls at parties. Their minds were a mess of scattered, hilariously contradictory "what ifs" and "I could nevers." They wanted to lead meaningful and fulfilling lives, bring something helpful and new into the world, and make some money to boot. Should be easy, right? But where on earth do you start?

Andrew, meanwhile, had a better idea of where he was going. He wanted to be a financial planner. Unfortunately, despite his vision and initial success, Andrew was lacking for good advice.

For that very reason, he had spent lunch with a major player in the finance industry. Encouraged by a friend, Andrew had phoned the man's office, explained he was a keen twenty-something, and set up a lunch. He left the meeting galvanized. The man had shared his entire life story, a tale replete with honesty and marvellous advice. Is that all it took? Was it as simple as phoning? Why had he always assumed it was so difficult to get people's attention? Perhaps successful people were more open to talking about their lives than he had assumed.

"We could write a book," Andrew exclaimed after regaling us with his story. "We could interview prominent Canadians, ask them how they got started, and write a book revealing the secrets of their success."

If you know Andrew, you know his energy is obnoxiously infectious. While the idea seemed like a long shot — why, for example, would these people want to participate in a book written by a bunch of nobodies? — Paul and Alex agreed.

Four days later, we met in Alex's parents' basement to brainstorm. Whom should we approach for an interview? We wanted to write a book about "successful" people, but what on earth did "success" mean? None of us could agree. Was money our yardstick? International recognition? Or maybe positive social impact? That sounded good, but how could you distinguish positive from negative without stumbling into the realm of subjective value judgments?

After much deliberation, we concluded that the word "success" applies to anyone who, by living according to his or her own personal dictates and desires, leaves a mark on the social fabric. Those who have agreed to participate in this book come from every corner of the country, a wide variety of fields, and myriad positions on the political spectrum. Some are incredibly wealthy; others are less so. Some believe in the market; others distrust it. In the end, what unites them is that, whether initially unsure, clear-eyed, or beset by hardships, all have left a mark on the world.

***

"If you get people on the phone," Andrew always contended, "they will talk with you." His dictum has proven true. From the half-hour cellphone conversation we had with Brian Mulroney to the meeting we had between beeper emergencies with cardiac surgeon Tirone David, the three of us have found our subjects remarkably accommodating.

Cartoonist Lynn Johnston invited us to her gorgeous lakeside studio outside of Corbeil, Ontario. After a five o'clock departure from Toronto, we embarked up the frozen Highway 400 and spent two hours awaiting a salt truck on an impassable stretch of northern roadway, only to arrive in time for a fantastic lunch and a three-hour interview. Johnston even asked if we'd like to stay the night. We would have loved to. Unfortunately, we had to work the next morning.

June Callwood met us for an hour-long coffee in the lobby of Raymond Moriyama's Toronto Reference Library. After insisting that we were all wasting our educations on such a ridiculous project, Callwood bristled at the notion that she was a feminist icon and then proceeded to mist up as she recalled her early days at *Maclean's* magazine. Then, with a nod and a cheeky smile, she darted like a flash across Yonge Street and receded into the crowds of her beloved city.

She knew she was ill. She knew the value of her time. And she didn't know us from Adam. We didn't have a publisher. We were just a bunch of goofy guys with a strange penchant for pestering famous Canadians. But June Callwood agreed to sit with us and give a small piece of herself to the book.

We were unknowns, and we knew it. But so long as we kept annoying people with phone calls, everyone was willing to grant us time. Matthew Coon Come agreed to an interview — provided we could catch him, that is. We repeatedly scheduled interviews with Coon Come, only to find a busy signal or pre-recorded message when we phoned him at the pre-arranged time.

The same held true for *Vanity Fair* editor Graydon Carter, whose gracious personal assistant — a young girl also hailing, surprisingly enough, from Toronto — became an almost daily phone date for a period of time in the middle of the project. As instructed, we would phone Carter's office at nine o'clock to suss out whether his schedule could accommodate a phone interview from his limousine between meetings and lunches. The answer was always the same: wait and see. So we would, until two or three in the afternoon, when we would phone again, only to find that tomorrow would probably work out better. Yes, tomorrow. Wonderful. And so the Beckettian farce continued. For months.

Perhaps it's because we've been convinced of the superior sheen of American success stories, or perhaps the Canadian sensibility makes us feel goofy about celebrating ourselves, but we live in a country where most people are flattered that anyone would want to ask questions of them. The few who refused to sit for our book did so because they felt they didn't deserve to be included in such a work. We kept insisting that the book wasn't a list of "great Canadians," but they humbly declined the opportunity nonetheless.

It sounds silly, but working on this book has helped instill in us a greater sense of what some in other countries might call patriotism, but we prefer to classify as simple appreciation. We appreciate that we live in a country that doesn't crow about itself, pat itself compulsively on the back, or grandstand on the international stage. Our self-effacing nature no doubt stems from inhabiting a colonial shadow, neighbouring a colossus, and living beside some of the most sublime and raw natural landscapes the planet has to offer. Canadians can't help but feel small in relation to the largest factors affecting our identity and culture.

***

In approaching participants, we wanted to ensure the book reflected not only a diversity of ages and backgrounds but also a diversity of approaches to the question of success. During the three years we worked on this project, we interviewed everyone from thirty-two-year-old virtuoso conductor Yannick Nézet-Séguin to seventy-nine-year-old billionaire Jim Pattison, from Olympic wrestler Daniel Igali to children's entertainer Raffi, from former B.C. premier and federal health minister Ujjal Dosanjh to award-winning filmmaker Patricia Rozema.

They say that the general reader is dead. They say that we all belong to microscopic niches rather than larger national or international communities; that an accountant can't learn from the story of a painter or vice versa; that someone in one region of the country has nothing in common with someone in another. We don't buy that argument for a second. And we hope, after you've read the incredible and diverse stories in this book, that you won't either.

***

Since beginning the project, we have been asked countless times about what we've gained from the experience. Many friends have suggested that the book needed an overarching idea, a lesson, or a self-help banner.

Yes, perhaps this would have sold better if we'd called it *The Seven Easy Steps to Success* or unearthed evidence that Canada's most successful citizens all happen to be descendants of the same alien species that crash landed somewhere in the middle of Saskatchewan in the 1920s.

Each of us has taken completely different advice and inspiration from the stories contained here. We're all remarkably different people, with remarkably different goals. As we knew when we began the book, success has nothing to do with filling swimming pools with money. It is a concept that only makes sense in relation to individual values and aspirations. To reduce the interviews we did to a few specific "keys to success" would be ridiculous. As a result, we've opted to present the stories in as bare and pure a form as possible. We let the interviewees — well over fifty of them — speak for themselves.

Finding a form that allowed us to do that was not easy. Magazine-style profiles give the reader the sense that they are accessing the subject through a filter. Raw interview transcripts, meanwhile, are over-long and littered with half-articulated thoughts. We sought a middle road, some way of giving the reader a lucid, unadulterated, and thoughtful set of stories.

The solution was to collaborate with our subjects. We shaped and refined their answers and then exchanged drafts with them until we had developed cohesive scripts that maintained the spirit of the initial interview while remaining tight and readable.

We hope the effect is much like sitting down for a quick coffee with our participants. Take from their stories what you will.

***

The subjects are divided into three groups: "Searchers," who took their time discovering what they wanted, "Survivors," who struggled against a variety of obstacles, and "Dreamers," who took alternative paths and made the universe conform to their will.

We felt it necessary to show that there is no single roadmap to success. Not everyone knew precisely what they wanted to do in their twenties. Few were able to simply side-step imposing and discouraging hurdles. It's easy to forget that the best things in life often require soul-searching, fortitude, and immense risk. Our participants serve as excellent reminders that quick fixes and easy answers rarely yield anything constructive or meaningful.

If there is one thing that connects the stories in this book, it's nerve. This isn't the typical quality we associate with Canadianness. Canadians always ask politely, always say "thank you," and follow even the most antiquated social protocols to a T. Right? Of course they do. Sometimes, though, they are pushy little buggers who take huge risks, refuse to fall into line, and stand up in the face of adversity and inequality.

If you want to play on the big stage, whether by starting a business, or making the art you want to make, or taking on suffering in the developing world, or entering the political arena, you need the nerve to take risks, demand attention, and ask for favours and advice.

For our generation — coddled from birth, largely unfamiliar with hardship, and cynical to a fault in a society where everything can be bought — this lesson is especially important. For all those living in their parents' basements or anxiously vacillating on the cusp of their potential, it is time to commit to something and push forward. When this project started, we too were crippled with questions. Though we've hardly found "The Answer," we've learned that to move forward we must start taking ownership of our own lives.

Politeness and grace are fantastic qualities and we should be glad we're associated with them. But just as you don't make friends with salad, you can't make a mark by waiting for your turn and avoiding confrontation. If Canadians are going to make a mark on the twenty-first century — and it would surely be a positive one — we'll no doubt need a little more nerve.

SEARCHERS

Canadians Who Took Their Time

JAMES ORBINSKI

"If you choose to work hard and make the lives of others slightly better, then you'll find your life will be more stimulating, interesting, and meaningful."

At seventeen, **James Orbinski** was your average confused, adventure-seeking teen. He twice abandoned his CEGEP studies in Montreal, first to head west and work in Alberta, and then to set up a hotel with his friends in the Laurentian Mountains. The same boldness that led him away from the classroom later took him to Africa, where his entire world view changed.

On a trip to Rwanda as a twenty-seven-year-old medical student, Orbinski realized that he had to respond to the misery being inflicted on the country. Upon returning home, he joined the Canadian branch of Médecins Sans Frontières (MSF) and went to work during the Somali civil war and the Rwandan genocide of the early 1990s. In 1999, as president of MSF's International Council, he accepted the Nobel Peace Prize on the organization's behalf. Since then, he has become an associate professor at the University of Toronto and the co-founder of Dignitas International, a humanitarian organization that implements community-based programs to fight HIV in Africa.

Early Exposure

When I was fourteen or fifteen, I had a job at an airport hotel. The place had a contract with Immigration Canada and part of the building was a detention centre for people held at the airport. Usually, these people had declared refugee status and were trying to enter the country without proper documentation. I was a short-order cook and waiter for the detainees. I would serve them food and then sit and listen as they talked about escaping from Guatemala or El Salvador. The experience taught me that life is not a movie and that the world "out there" is also "in here," in my space, in my life.

One teacher in high school — a man named Michael Lieberman — was profoundly influential in this regard. He nurtured a sense that everyone must be "able to respond" and, therefore, "response-able" or "responsible." He taught me that our values matter, that they are the beginning of whatever enterprise we undertake. Through him and others, I slowly understood the importance of choice. The exercise of choice is our greatest responsibility as human beings. We all have to choose how we're going to be in the world. That, more than any information I acquired in high school, left a serious mark.

University Days

When it came time to apply to university, I was looking for something multidisciplinary: a place where I could spend time outside; a place where I'd be treated as a person rather than a number. I had no firm idea of what I wanted to do. I just wanted to learn as much as I could.

What sold me on Trent University was the recruiter. He was sincere, he wasn't pretentious, and he seemed genuinely interested in me. He wasn't trying to sell me anything. He was just trying to help me find the right place. I just felt that if this was the kind of person they chose to represent the university, then that was the place I wanted to go.

Besides, I'd always had this fantasy about the Trent-Severn Waterway. I'd never been there, but I'd read about it in brochures. "Wow," I used to say. "Look at those rivers. I'm going to canoe to school every day!"

Trent was a wonderful place. It had a collegiate system and small tutorials where you received close academic attention. It was also contemporary. They were doing Native and environmental studies when no other universities would touch those subjects. There was a religious zeal about ensuring that every student had a solid arts and science background by the end of the first two years. You weren't allowed to specialize until your third year. Education was about exposure.

I studied experimental theatre, environmental science, biochemistry, phenomenology, accounting, and computer science. "Blake, Shelley and Keats" was one of my favourite courses, as were "Irish and English Literature" and "Canadian Literature." I guess I was trying to understand my place in the world and my cultural background, in terms of current political realities, my family history, and, having come to Canada from England at the age of nine, being an immigrant. Feeling Canadian only came slowly — it came through a process of inquiry and constant questioning.

In the end, I majored in psychology. I loved all the deep philosophical questions that emerged in psychology class: "What is the self?" "What is the other?" "Can you alter perception?" All that fascinated me. I would listen to one professor talk about the existential implications of the phenomenology of perception. The next hour I would listen to someone tell me that was bullshit, and all that mattered was what could be measured, walking us through the lessons of chi-square distribution.

What's Your Question?

The whole time, I was exploring with intent. It wasn't just an orgy of passions and ideas. I knew that I was interested in clinical psychology and that I wanted to enter some kind of concrete profession.

Oftentimes, people assume there's a map, one algorithmic answer to life. I see it a lot in students, especially with the phenomenon of résumés — everyone's a volunteer, everyone's saving the world, everyone's a superhero, and they get A+ in every course. Students come and ask me what they should do, and implicit in their questions is the idea that there's a right way of going through the steps, that if they're not following the map, they're missing out.

There is no map. Everyone needs to find what excites and intrigues them. The issue is not "what's *the* question?" but "what's *your* question?"

In my experience, that question changed. It would lead me in a direction, and then I'd get an answer and be forced to change tracks. Coming out of university, it was, "Do I want to pursue clinical psychology?" That question landed me in a high-security youth detention centre in Calgary.

I was a youth worker there. The adolescents were being held in custody while awaiting either a court date or a custody order. They were mostly street kids who had been involved in prostitution, drug sales, or violence. When I sat and talked to them, I came to see that the vast majority of them had been either sexually or physically abused, neglected, or forced from their homes.

A lot of what we did ended up being a form of counselling: helping kids think about their overall direction in life and getting them access, if necessary, to psychologists.

Changing Tracks

Ultimately, I realized that counselling wasn't a great fit for me. I don't want to minimize the importance of psychology, but I found that, in my experience, it was entirely too technical. It overlooked the genuineness that can exist between two people. It imposed a set of technical skills, tools, and models on all interactions.

I also felt that I needed something practical. I thought medicine would be the best profession to pursue because, though requiring a deep knowledge base, it was also very practical. I felt that I could remain myself as a physician. My time at the detention centre had helped me understand that.

In the end, I applied to medical school. I thought that the program at McMaster University would be the best fit — and it was. It was problem-based learning, with small tutorials, self-evaluations, real patients, real problems, and no lectures. The first week, I was presented with the case of a five-year-old boy who came to his doctor with an ear infection, received treatment, and returned three days later with meningitis. Right away, I had to learn about the interior workings of the ear, the anatomy of the neck, why the infection would pass from the ear to the nervous system, and what an immune system was. I was acquiring knowledge in a very practical way.

Working in Rwanda

I fell in love with immunology in my first week of med school, mainly because it seemed as though no one knew much about it. I loved how confusing and challenging it was. The biggest thing in the area of immunology was AIDS, especially pediatric AIDS. No one knew a thing. In my third year, Dick Newfeld, the associate dean and my medical advisor, pushed me to pursue the issue and apply for a fellowship with the Medical Research Council of Canada and the International Development Research Centre. The fellowship involved going to the main hospital in Kigali, Rwanda.

I did it for the adventure more than anything. Africa was a huge mystery. "You're adding another year," a lot of people said. "What are you going to learn? What does this have to do with medicine? It's crazy!" But many were supportive too.

When I arrived in Rwanda, I realized just how unprepared I was. I didn't even understand that politics like that were possible. Beneath the surface, it was a very different, dark culture. At the time, the development mantra was pervasive among aid workers: "Everyone's developing and the West is great." That was the dominant feeling at the time. There was a strong sense of post-colonial superiority to it all. But it was a very hopeful time too.

I was twenty-seven and very idealistic. That hasn't changed. I'm still very hopeful about the world. Once you see that there are other ways of living, that there are good and bad politics, then you can choose to respond. What's your choice? If you choose cynicism, despair, and self-indulgence, then you get what you choose. If you choose to work hard and make the lives of others slightly better, then you'll find your life will be more stimulating, interesting, and meaningful.

Discovering Médecins Sans Frontières

My experience in Rwanda completely changed my life. I suddenly knew that pediatric immunology and the study of infectious diseases weren't going to cut it. Not for me. As fascinating as they were, there were people far better at it than I was. I liked it, but I didn't *love* it anymore. I knew I had to do something else to help ease the suffering I'd seen.

Before going to Rwanda, I had never heard of Médecins Sans Frontières. There was no website because there was no Internet. I met a couple of its aid workers at a party in Rwanda. But since the organization wasn't actually working in the country at the time, that was the only exposure I had. When I came back, a guy at med school named Richard Heinzl knew more about MSF and was interested in starting a Canadian chapter. I jumped at the opportunity to join.

Médecins Sans Frontières brought a significant change to humanitarianism. It broke all the rules, shattering everyone's conceptions of neutrality. By proceeding in the way it did, the organization proclaimed that there are certain circumstances under which one can no longer be neutral. That was bold and that's what I gravitated towards.

Getting Out of Debt

Coming out of med school, I had a lot of debt to pay off. You've got to be somewhat mercenary about how you approach your finances, especially in our society. I didn't want anything pulling me down the traditional path so many other doctors were following. The best way to do that was to work damned hard for a few years.

I was working as a locum in Orangeville while the doctor I was replacing was sick. Unfortunately, he ultimately died. I had no intention of buying the practice, but there was a demand, so, in the end, I did.

I was living in Toronto's St. Lawrence Market area at the time MSF Canada was getting off the ground. You have a lot of flexibility when you own a practice. You can close for an afternoon or take a morning off. It was essential to be able to take time to work on MSF. Without the Orangeville practice, I never would have been able to ditch my debts and fully commit to such a time-consuming initiative.

Finding a Path

You don't do humanitarian work to win a prize. You do it because you must — because you have no other choice. I'd always tried to figure out my place in the world. After a while, I realized that I had no choice. I knew that, however futile it seemed, it was better to take that extreme step than to wallow in despair or acquiescence. So I forged on.

MARGOT FRANSSEN

"Because we didn't know what could go wrong, we just kept moving forward with as much energy as we could muster."

When **Margot Franssen** left York University with a philosophy degree in 1979, she had no idea what lay in store. Five years later, along with husband Quig Tingley and sister Betty-Ann, she brought The Body Shop to Canada and oversaw one of the British cosmetic chain's most profitable markets. It set a benchmark for combining retail savvy with social activism. As president of the company, she stood behind her promise never to test on animals, while vigorously campaigning for the environment and human rights long before those causes became chic among CEOs.

After selling the Canadian rights back to the parent company in 2004, Franssen immediately set up Accessorize, a women's accessory chain, with eleven stores across three provinces. An Officer of the Order of Canada and a recipient of the United Nations Grand Award for fighting violence against women, Franssen also serves on the board of the CIBC and the Women's College Hospital and is president of the Canadian Women's Foundation.

Glass Ceilings

In 1954, when I was two years old, my parents and I emigrated from Holland. Although my father was trained as a mechanical engineer, no one in Canada would accept his degree, so he and my mom were forced to start from scratch. He learned English, pumped gas, and went to night school, while my mom cleaned houses. I remember a time when there wasn't enough food to eat, but my parents' determination to make a good home for my sister and me was a real inspiration. I watched them slowly and steadily climb the ladder to the middle class.

When I was eighteen, we were living in Lethbridge, Alberta. I desperately wanted to be in Toronto. I yearned for the bustle and liveliness of the big city. The second I finished high school, I hopped on a train to Toronto in search of a job. I found a rooming house where I shared a bathroom with six girls and a kitchen with four, and paid $12 a week in rent. I was happy as a clam.

Having already worked in retail throughout my teenage years, I decided to look for an office job. Though confident in myself, I had no marketable skills. I had to fib on all my applications, claiming I could clerk and type.

Miraculously, I landed a job at an investment firm called McLeod Young Weir. I posted retail stock sales and made coffee for $80 a week. I watched these young men come through the office as part of the training program and I'd say to myself, "I could do that. I'm easily as smart as they are." But when I asked about the program, my boss just laughed. "We don't pay for women to do that," he said. "They wouldn't pass." The culture at McLeod Young Weir was clearly defined: I would be left posting stock sales forever. I said, "Too bad, your loss," and left.

My next job was as a secretary in the human resources department at a mutual fund company. I interviewed women and was required to ask the most bizarre and appalling questions: "What is the state of your marriage?" "Does your husband allow you to work?" "What kind of birth control are you using?" Those were the standard legal questions in the 1970s. I couldn't stand it, so I left again.

Then I got a job as a personal assistant at another investment firm. After I kept bugging them, the company finally paid for me to take the Investment Dealers Association course. I was amazed, thinking I was finally going to be allowed to trade. I passed the first and the second tests easily. On the third test, I even had higher marks than the president of the company, who was taking it at the same time. After each one, I approached management and asked if I could trade. The answer was always the same: "Maybe next year." One day, I stepped back, took stock of myself, and realized I couldn't wait for others to allow me to achieve my goal. I had watched my mother

In those days, being the only Chinese-Canadian in the CFL was kind of a novelty. I didn't receive any adverse treatment from my teammates. It was a different story in public places and in other cities, though, especially at some of the big hotels and stores we used to go to — or tried to go to. We weren't made to feel very welcome. It wasn't something they made a big point of, but you could still feel it. Only when people learned I was a first-string player and had made some of the all-star teams did I begin to earn their respect. But it took time.

— **Normie Kwong**, Lieutenant-Governor of Alberta, former CFL halfback for the Calgary Stampeders and the Edmonton Eskimos, the youngest player to win a Grey Cup, and, upon retirement, the holder of thirty league records and father fight their way through hardship. I wasn't going to let anyone hold me back.

The Paper Chase

I knew I would never get ahead without more education, so I enrolled in business courses at York University. The only way to justify starting a bachelor's degree at twenty-three was to have a clearly defined goal: mine was to end with a job in hand.

The first few months of classes were horrible. The study of business was excruciatingly boring. One day, I met a student who seemed really passionate about the university experience. I asked him what he studied. He said he was majoring in philosophy. "What's that?" I asked. I had literally no idea. When he started talking about the various branches of philosophy and the questions they sought to answer, bells began ringing in my head. I thought it sounded like the most intriguing thing in the world. I quickly switched my major.

I knew a philosophy degree would be practically worthless and wouldn't help me get a job. But I was so happy to find something I could be passionate about. Over the next three and a half years, I fell in love with academics. The difference between high school and university was staggering. Suddenly, I became a new type of student: one who actually enjoyed learning.

The Gift

Since I was living with my boyfriend, Quig, I was lucky enough to have the security of a roof over my head and food on the table. That said, I still worked part-time as an assistant to sculptor Maryon Kantaroff. She was a remarkable person who introduced me to the world of feminism and the women fighting for equality. I had never come into intimate contact with feminism before, but everything they said reverberated with me. My experience over the previous four years was proof that these women were right: change was necessary.

When I graduated from university, Maryon bought me a present. It was a gift basket from a new store called The Body Shop, which she had discovered while working in England. I was grateful for the gift but didn't really use all the products. "Thank you," I said, putting it aside. Later, knowing she would ask me if I liked it, I decided to open the basket. The cosmetic bottles inside were the ugliest things I had ever seen! They looked like urine samples. I was intrigued — not so much by the products themselves, but by the packaging. I went back to Maryon and asked about the store. "It's like an apothecary's shop," she told me. "A refill bar on one side and a perfume bar on the other."

I needed a job. I didn't want to go to graduate school, and with a philosophy degree I couldn't do much else. My mind began rushing ahead of me, thinking about what I might be able to do with a business like The Body Shop in Canada.

Taking a Leap

Quig gave me the plane fare to go and see what The Body Shop was actually like. I flew to London with a flight attendant friend who could travel for free. Our intention was to copy the idea and bring it back to Canada.

The company was still fairly small: they had been running for three years and only had six locations. My friend and I rented a car and drove around to every store. Every time we walked in, I felt like I was hearing a song I already knew, a tune I could hum even if I didn't know the words. In hindsight, I realize it was the corporate culture I was responding to. I was intrigued enough to phone Anita and Gordon Roddick, the store's founders, and ask if we could discuss expanding into Canada.

I had lunch with Anita, who then invited me for dinner that evening. Initially, I said no — I'm not sure why — but she pushed me until I agreed.

When I knocked at their door, a little girl answered. I announced that I was there to see her parents. "You must be the lady from Canada," she chirped. "I expect that after dining with us you'll want children of your own!" I was shocked. Who were these people?

That evening, Anita, Gordon, and I drank the only thing in the house — cheap brandy. A lot of cheap brandy. We talked and talked through the evening. They didn't know that I was bullshitting my way through the whole night. I just made up my knowledge of marketing, retailing, and cosmetics. Little did I know that they were bullshitting too, pretending to know about franchising and North America. They had never been to North America and had only franchised twice. They didn't have a clue.

Eventually, it was too late for me to go home, so they offered me the guest bedroom. Before we said goodnight, Gordon asked, "What exactly do you want?" I felt that since I was standing on thin ice I might as well dance. "I'm not interested in owning one little shop," I said. "I want all of Canada or nothing." To my horror and delight, he said, "Okay, you've got it." The next morning, we shook hands on the deal. I flew home and said to Quig, "This is it! We're starting a business!"

The Body Shop in Canada

At the beginning, The Body Shop Canada was composed of Quig, my sister Betty-Ann, and myself. He kept his job as a bond trader and director at McLeod Young Weir — thank God for the security! Betty-Ann and I scouted for locations and built the first store with a contractor — hammering, stripping, and painting. Since I was more familiar with being a customer than a business owner, our only guiding principle was that we would run the store from the customer's perspective.

For the first ten years, our franchise agreement with Anita and Gordon was based on a handshake. Our lawyers were appalled that we rejected legal documents. They kept asking us to make it legally binding. "We like the way they think," we told them. "We don't need a piece of paper. Our relationship is based on trust."

Because the three of us were doing everything ourselves — even cleaning the toilets — our overhead was low and the first store was breaking even within six months. We even sold our first franchise around that time. A woman walked into the store and asked if we franchised. I said no, but my sister kicked me under the table and said, "Yes, as a matter of fact, we do." When the woman asked how much it would cost, I had to make up an amount on the spot. I knew we owed the bank $5,000. I wanted to pay that off as soon as possible. "Five thousand dollars," I told her.

The woman asked where we wanted the franchise located. We told her to look anywhere she could, figuring it would take her as long as it had taken us. Within a week, she was back, having found a location in Toronto's Eaton Centre. When it came time to negotiate the lease, I had no idea what I was doing. I faked it because I wanted my franchisees to be confident in our abilities.

When the tenant subletting the space in the Eaton Centre said we would have to pay $20,000 extra for the carpet and cash desk, I had no idea he was actually asking for "key money" — essentially a payout on the side. I had never leased a mall property before and it seemed he was being extremely unreasonable. "Are you crazy?" I asked. "This carpet is crap and the desk is in horrible shape. I'm not giving you a cent for that!" He must have thought I was insane. Worried that I would reveal his demand to the mall, he said, "Okay, lady. You can have it for nothing." If I had known what key money was, I would have negotiated. My ignorance allowed me to get the spot for nothing.

That's how it went for the first few years. We were blindly feeling our way along. Because we didn't know what could go wrong, we just kept moving forward with as much energy as we could muster. The stores kept opening up, one after another, until eventually there were 130 across the country producing $130 million of retail sales per year.

Throughout those years, work was my life. Having been impeded so much before going to university, I was determined to build The Body Shop into a business that was both a financial success and a reflection of our values. We succeeded because we were filling a niche in the marketplace. People loved that we had brought ethics into business; they sensed we were proceeding with integrity. Those ethics grew directly out of who we were as human beings and from what mattered most to us. Consumers could see that our corporate culture wasn't phony or part of a marketing program. It was simply us.

MARK ROWSWELL

*"No single person can change an entire social system by himself.
But I figured I could use the Dashan phenomenon to open a few minds."*

Hailing from a middle-class neighbourhood in Ottawa, **Mark Rowswell** didn't travel much as a teenager. He was an average student who showed no special ability in foreign languages. However, he always dreamed of getting away.

Now, under his pseudonym, "Dashan," he has become the most famous foreigner in China. Though he first made his name as a comedic performer, he is better known as the host of educational shows, cultural events, and entertainment programs, including one for Chinese New Year that reaches a staggering 500 million viewers. Lately, he has expanded into dramatic acting on both television and stage. Renowned for his astonishing grasp of Mandarin and Chinese humour, Dashan is proof that curiosity and commitment can take us anywhere.

Languages

At the end of Grade 12, a nascent interest in photography led me to take a job at a one-hour photo store. One of my co-workers was a Chinese-Canadian, and she started teaching me Cantonese when business was slow. At first, I learned a few phrases just to freak out the Chinese customers.

I had just dropped French. It had been compulsory up to Grade 12, but I had never liked it. However, I soon began to regret not being able to speak a foreign language. Many of my friends were from immigrant families and they could speak all kinds of languages. French and the other European languages didn't have much allure to me. They seemed too boring and "old world." I wanted to learn Swahili, Tagalog, Urdu, or something.

Chinese seemed like a good idea. It was foreign and exotic enough. There was even a chance it might be useful one day. But practical considerations didn't really concern me. I just wanted to learn something about a part of the world that was as far away from mine as possible.

East Asian Studies

I decided to attend the University of Toronto because it was in a big city and it afforded me the chance to get away from home. It was the only comprehensive university in the downtown area. I didn't care what school I was at, provided I was in a stimulating environment. I believed, as I still do, that it's the student who determines the quality of education.

At the time, I wasn't thinking about getting specific job training. Studying commerce in university just so that you could get a job in business struck me as incredibly boring. I was looking to expand my mind, complete a general education, and become a knowledgeable and engaged member of society. I'd worry about finding a career later.

In first year, I took a broad range of courses, keeping my options open. I started taking courses in Chinese, this time in the national dialect, Mandarin, because Cantonese is not taught formally in universities. I enjoyed the courses so much I decided to take Mandarin as a major. I also began to feel that I needed to belong to a smaller community. The East Asian Studies department became just that.

As time went on, I became more and more immersed in studying the Chinese language and culture. I spent one summer working at the Toronto office of a state-run Chinese trading company. The next year, I travelled to Taiwan, Hong Kong, and mainland China. By the end, my Mandarin was quite good. I had gone from being a B+ student in high school to a highly regarded A student.

I learned a couple of lessons very early on. First, you always have to out-work the competition. When I was in my twenties, I realized that most people didn't work weekends. If I was going to succeed, Saturdays and Sundays had to become workdays. The second lesson was that cash was king. Because it was impossible to control my revenue, I had to control my overhead and my debt. Banks don't take risks. When I would ask for a loan, I started to under-promise and overachieve. Banks will only lend money if you can prove you don't need it.

— **Ron Foxcroft**, Canada's first NCAA basketball referee and the inventor of the Fox 40 Whistle, used in sporting events across the globe

A Year at Beijing University

When I finished my degree, I wasn't quite ready to start searching for a career. I felt I needed to spend six months to a year in China to wind up that stage in my life. I thought I owed it to myself to try to use what I had learned in Canada and immerse myself in Chinese culture. After six months, I could figure out whether I wanted to continue in this direction or find something new.

I applied for a federal government scholarship, the Canadian-China Scholarly Exchange Program. They accepted me and sent me to Beijing University for one year, automatically renewable for a second.

My Mandarin was good enough to read a newspaper and navigate daily conversations. I was so excited about finally living abroad that I didn't worry about how I would fare. I didn't

Mark Rowswell (Dashan): "I just wanted to learn something about a part of the world that was as far away as possible."

care that I didn't know anyone. I was looking for adventure, not comfort. As for the politics of the country, I wasn't that concerned. There had been student protests a year or two before, but — to be honest — I was actually hoping to see some first-hand.

In the end, things worked out better than I'd expected. The fact that I'd travelled in China two years before helped a lot. Travelling on a shoestring budget is much harder than setting up in a university dorm. I found campus life relatively easy. Besides, at the beginning, the novelty was what I was there for. The culture shock only starts when that begins to wear off. Luckily, for me, it never really did.

I was living in something of a foreign ghetto inside Beijing University. There were over six hundred foreigners in that area and they constituted a small community unto themselves. We had our own dorms, our own cafeteria, our own shops, and our own bars. Even though I was attending classes with Chinese students, there was little interaction. We lived in separate worlds.

Luckily, through sheer force of will, I was able to break out of this insular community. I gradually stopped eating at the foreign students' cafeteria and started actively making friends with Chinese students.

Getting on Television

Among the foreign students, my Chinese was better than average. Most had only done a year or two of Chinese in their home countries. I, on the other hand, had already done a four-year BA.

One day, a Chinese TV producer came to the university looking for a foreigner who could speak Mandarin. They wanted someone to host an international singing competition. One of the teachers recommended me. I went along for the experience. I wanted to get off campus and see a different side of the country.

The first show led to the second. A month later, I was invited to perform a comedy skit on national television during a New Year's Eve special. Five hundred and fifty million people were going to be watching!

In the skit, I played a character called "Dashan," which means "big mountain" (I'm rather tall). The response was amazing. I became a star virtually overnight. That's why, in China, I'm still known as Dashan. Suddenly all kinds of opportunities began to open up. Each show was a new experience that helped broaden my understanding of the country.

At first I was simply a novelty act. People were astounded that a foreigner could speak the vernacular language of daily life rather than just the formal language they taught at school.

Being Initiated into the Art of *Xiangsheng*

During that New Year's show, I met Jiang Kun. He was a master of *xiangsheng*, the Chinese art of linguistic play and comedic language. *Xiangsheng* is basically like stand-up comedy, though the most common form is the two-man dialogue. Each act is centred on one specific topic, story, or theme. You simply riff on that. The humour typically comes from the use of puns, double meanings, and linguistic tricks. Cultural references are hugely important as well.

Jiang Kun was part of the golden generation of *xiangsheng*, directly after the end of the Cultural Revolution in 1976. He was and remains the most famous practitioner of the art.

Later that year, Jiang Kun and I got together a few more times. I was interested in *xiangsheng* and he was interested in me. He formally accepted me as his pupil in November, almost a full year after the initial show.

Studying *xiangsheng* is primarily done one sketch at a time. You learn one performance, do it on stage repeatedly, and continue to polish it. At the beginning, you learn standard skits that everybody knows. With these, there is a very clear precedent to imitate. Eventually, you write your own.

For the next New Year's show, Jiang Kun and I performed together in a skit called "Famous Teacher, Bright Apprentice." That was the first real *xiangsheng* I had done. A big part of the humour was simply the fact that a foreigner could say what I was saying. I would consistently get the better of Jiang Kun, demonstrating a deeper understanding of the language and culture. The audience could not believe what they were hearing.

Breaking the Mould

Dashan's reputation grew exponentially. Working with Jiang Kun gave me a legitimate position within performing circles. I was no longer just a foreign guest. Most foreign performers in China find it very difficult (if not impossible) to break out of the established mould. It's perfectly understandable when you think about it. It's only recently that the media industry in the West has treated blacks and Asians with any sort of equality and respect. And that's within multicultural societies. Ninety-five percent of China is from the same ethnic group. Foreigners represent only a tiny slice of society.

My increasing popularity allowed me the freedom to make choices about what projects to undertake. If the media wanted a foreigner, they could choose anyone. If they wanted Dashan, I could use my leverage to determine what kind of work I'd be doing.

I gradually figured out what I wanted Dashan's image to be. I didn't really get any help in this regard. I'm the kind of person who listens to anybody's advice but won't necessarily agree with it. I don't feel a strong need to persuade others, so I just go ahead quietly in my own way. I have a very strong independent streak.

I was convinced that the best way to change the image of foreigners in the Chinese media was simply to be true to myself and to avoid playing into negative stereotypes. Sidney Poitier made a name for himself in the 1960s because he played roles that were not traditionally associated with the stereotypical image of African-Americans. No single person can change an entire social system by himself. But I figured I could use the Dashan phenomenon to open a few minds.

I ended up staying at Beijing University for three years instead of one or two. Being a student definitely took a back seat to everything else. It was pretty clear that my understanding of the country was benefiting from my performance work and my travels. If I wanted to sit in a room and cram information into my brain, I could have stayed at home.

Not Ready to Return

When my time at university was over, I wasn't ready to head home. With the help of the Canadian Embassy I got three years of work experience. The ambassador personally hired me to work on cultural and academic affairs, and then on public issues in general, helping to promote the knowledge and understanding of Canada in China. It was all contract work, so provided I fulfilled the terms, I could do whatever I wanted on the side. Besides performing, I did consulting work for various companies and helped promote Canadian businesses — in the role of Dashan.

In 1995, after three years at the embassy, I left to do full-time freelance work as Dashan. At that point, I returned to Ontario and registered Dashan Inc. It was a risky move, seeing as I now had a wife and a child. It ended up being quite stressful at first, but the gamble paid off.

For me, success is freedom: the freedom to live your life the way you choose. It also means providing that level of freedom to your wife and kids. We don't live in luxury, but we have everything we need, as well as a considerable safety net to fall back on.

It would be extremely rare for a Canadian student to come to China assuming they'll never return to Canada. When I arrived, I expected to leave in two years. That turned into seven. Now, though I return home all the time, I've made a life for myself in China.

The path I've taken has been a strange one, and it's certainly not something I planned. It was all done one step at a time, taking things as they came, while trying to keep an eye open for long-term considerations. Looking back, it's hard to imagine it any other way.

"Sometimes I think that success is a biochemical accident — it's all reliant on energy. Either you're willing to put in the time or you aren't."

Patricia Rozema shocked the country, and herself, when her first feature film, *I've Heard the Mermaids Singing*, won La Prix de la Jeunesse at the Cannes International Film Festival in 1987. In the wake of Cannes, Harvey Weinstein of Miramax came calling, and the film became an international indie hit. Rozema has since gone on to direct the Golden Bear–nominated *When Night is Falling*, a critically acclaimed adaptation of Jane Austen's *Mansfield Park*, an instalment of the Emmy Award–winning TV series *Yo-Yo Ma Inspired by Bach*, episodes of HBO's groundbreaking series *Tell Me You Love Me*, and the upcoming *Kit Kittredge: An American Girl Mystery*.

But Rozema was never one of those people who grew up yearning to direct. In fact, television and films were barred from her strict Dutch Calvinist home. In her teens, Rozema went through what she calls "a religious phase," during which she attempted to convert everyone she met. Her desire to affect others led her to consider acting and journalism while at university. All the while, though, she was marked by what she calls a "fictive impulse," a desire to create new worlds.

The Sloppy Journalist

Going into journalism seemed like a good idea. "Here's a viable way of making money by telling stories," I thought. "I'll meet people who have the power to change the world or are at the centre of crises. I'll tell their stories and I'll get paid for it." I knew I'd probably go on to work on my own stories on the side, but I needed a marketable skill.

It worked out for a while. When I finished my undergraduate degree, with a major in English literature and philosophy and a minor in journalism, I did practicums at radio stations. That's when I discovered images. It was a struggle to fight myself away from words and radio, but images have such undeniable power. Show a thousand different people an image and you'll be faced with a thousand different opinions. Once I discovered that, journalism wasn't just a day job anymore. Now it was everything. When I was twenty-three, I found out that the CBC was prepping a new current affairs show called *The Journal*. I jumped at the opportunity.

I got a job as an associate producer. They only called me that because they didn't want to call me a researcher. But that's what I was — a researcher. The producers would come to me and say, "The U.S. is about to start testing cruise missiles over Alberta. Do a piece on cruise missiles." Then I'd amass all the footage we had of cruise missiles, get all the information I could about the story, write a script, and then cut a piece about it. The senior editors would take what I had, edit it, and air it. It was fantastic.

The problem was that I felt insecure as a journalist. I'm not a born journalist. You need to have an encyclopedic mind and an obsessive attention to detail. I was sloppy. I'd always think about how I could change the details of the story to make it more moving or interesting. Since I was a kid, I've possessed a "fictive impulse," an inexplicable desire to make people believe in different realities. Working in journalism, that impulse kept rearing its head.

When I wasn't thinking about how to mess with the story, I would get facts wrong. I didn't know anything about Canadian history. I had gone to a Dutch Calvinist school that focused predominantly on theology. I had no idea who the power families in Canada were. I just wasn't suited for the job.

I got sick of interviewing other people and focusing on what they were doing. I wanted to be the one doing something. I knew that I wanted to make something and I grew increasingly frustrated with how little time I had to do anything outside of work.

Making a Film

At the time, I was completely in love with film. It was the era of the first big influx of European and American art films in Canada. I was watching Bergman, Truffaut, Buñuel, Fellini, Cassavetes, and Woody Allen. I wanted to start a cinema review where I would write about all the wonderful films I was seeing.

During one period, I had three weeks of vacation from *The Journal*. I decided I would try to make a short film. From what I remember, it was going to be a satire of a self-help video. It was going to feature mannequins learning to say their names and make friends. I tried to raise money but I couldn't. I didn't realize that you can't raise money, shoot, edit, and finish a film in three weeks. It was really discouraging.

Soon after I returned from my vacation, *The Journal* fired me. The budget had to be trimmed and I was low on the totem pole. Besides, I had started to bug people. I was a bit too artsy for *The Journal*. I remember trying to convince them to do a story on Laurie Anderson's "O Superman." There I was, sitting in front of twenty-five of Canada's top journalists, playing this supremely slow, experimental song. They just stared at me. I don't know what possessed me to think they would get it.

Once I was fired, I didn't have a clue what to do. As I've already said, I'm a crazy overachiever. To be fired was way too much to handle. Finally it occurred to me to give film a shot. I would never have imagined making a living in film, but I just wanted to see if I had the goods. So I went on what they used to call unemployment insurance — they call it employment insurance now — and sat at my desk every day and wrote. Most of what I produced was dreck. I'd apply for grants and get rejected. But I persevered. I was on a mission. Finally, I got a grant for a short script I'd written.

An Ambivalent Relationship with the Rules

During this period, I was systematic about taking everybody I knew who was even remotely related to the film business out for coffee. "What do you do?" I'd ask. "Who gives you money? And what do you have to do to get it?" Finally, someone told me to go and see Peter Mettler. He had just finished shooting something and apparently had a really cool look. So I tracked him down at Ryerson, where he taught. He was one of the most beautiful people I had ever met. The thing he'd just shot was by some guy named Atom Egoyan. "Hurry," he said. "See it at the Carlton Cinema, because it'll be gone soon." It was called *Next of Kin* and it was terrific. So I got Atom's phone number and called him in Victoria. I asked where he got his money from and how he went about making his film. He laughed. Here I was, some chick phoning from Toronto, asking about how to make a movie.

I treated it like research. I got every book I could on screenwriting and directing. When I wrote, I would spill uncontrollably onto the page. The first draft would be an emotional mess, then I would apply the rules when things weren't working. I would pull out the red pencil and try to give the story a shape.

I had an ambivalent relationship with the rules. I was insistent that my film wouldn't look like every other film I'd seen. I didn't want it to be an ordinary narrative. There are two types of writers: filmmakers and artists — those who respond to art and those who respond to life. I didn't have enough of a film education to respond to art, even if I'd wanted to. I was responding to life and life alone. I wanted to capture the feelings I was tapping into as I wrote. That said, whenever I thought the script seemed inexplicably flat or boring, I'd look at the books. They'd say things like, "If you haven't introduced a turn by this many pages, people are going to start feeling that you've repeated the same dynamic too many times. You'll need to switch things up." I'd read that, realize the author was right, and make a change.

Assistant Directing

During this period, I also pursued a lot of assistant directing work. From working at *The Journal*, I knew a director named Don Owen who had made one of Canada's first recognizable features, a film called *Nobody Waved Goodbye*. I begged him to take me on as his assistant. I told him I'd work for free and he agreed. But he was bad. He didn't do his homework. He was never ready for the day's shooting; he'd write the scenes that morning. That was how he had worked before and everyone had loved it, so he saw no need to change. But working with him made me realize that, if I had the money, I would do it better.

Later, I did assistant directing for David Cronenberg as well. He had the most civilized, gentle, and intelligent manner, the most un-neurotic way of working. I found that very encouraging, though I didn't really like the extremity of his work at the time. I remember standing outside the door to a hospital room while he was delivering Geena Davis's maggot baby in *The Fly*. She was screaming and I saw this maggot baby and somehow it all seemed so foul. I had a real crisis. "What the hell am I doing here?" I thought. "I didn't get into the business to do this." The scene made a lot more sense when I saw it on screen, though.

I never really gravitated to Cronenberg's content, but I learned a great deal from the way he worked. That's what I've always found: I discover process from colleagues, but in terms of content, there are only a handful of films that I'd want to emulate.

First Time Directing: *Passion: A Letter in 16mm*

When I finally had the money for the film, I felt quite confident about directing. All I had to do was visualize what I wanted and then describe it. I knew I had to get the best possible people around me. If you get people who impress the hell out of you and have the same default mode as you, then all you have to do is keep describing. As long as you're working to get everything right, you're hard on yourself, and you don't piss them off, you'll get their best work.

The biggest surprise once the film was done was that you get what you see. When I set out, I honestly believed that if you put a camera on two men sitting and talking, the footage would be something more than just two guys sitting and talking. I think that comes from our post–Industrial Revolution faith in technology. We just assume that the camera is going to lift things up to an entirely new level. But you have to be doing something extraordinary in front of the camera, because the camera won't save you.

The other thing that surprised me was that others shared my sensibilities. When people saw the movie, they responded to it in such a way that I felt less alone. I always thought I had a very private sense of humour. I'd really just been making the movie for myself. That whole process helped me understand that, if I pleased myself, I had a better chance of pleasing others.

In some ways, the first film was the easiest. It gets much harder once you get older, because then you have something to lose. Your first film is a piece of cake. No one is expecting anything from you. That first piece is just you, driven by all the things that have made you who you are. Your second film: that's a struggle. Because then

Patricia Rozema: "Your first film is a piece of cake. No one is expecting anything from you."

it's "Oh god, everyone's watching and it's important. Be free, be free. But don't repeat yourself. And don't go too far away from what you do really well." You become so spectacularly self-conscious and you clench up.

Advice

When I'm talking to young people, I always say, "Do your homework and listen to your gut." A lot of people who listen to their gut and then tell everyone to screw off won't necessarily go to the ends of the earth to get things done properly. If you're going to go and talk to someone, make sure you know everything there is to know about them. If you're going to do something, do it right. Few people do that. Sometimes I think that success is a biochemical accident — it's all reliant on energy. Either you're willing to put in the time or you aren't.

CHRISTOPHER PRATT

*"I recognized the limitations of confining myself to an
environment like the Maritimes. I was never able to have
knock 'em dead conversations with other painters."*

Christopher Pratt is one of Canada's best-known and most beloved painters. His meticulous prints depict the stark landscapes
of his native Newfoundland and explore the province's ambivalent relationship with modernity. His work is synonymous with Newfoundland; in 1980, he even designed the province's new flag.

But Pratt wasn't always going to be a painter. Growing up,
he never considered painting a possibility. He knew of no professional painters or art galleries in Newfoundland. Then, after
he had his appendix out as a teenager, his parents bought him
water paints, paper, and brushes to let him pass the time until
recovery. Confined to his back garden, Pratt's mind fled back to
a trout-fishing excursion he'd taken with his father the previous
year. He painted a particular spot on the river as he saw it in his
mind. With that, Pratt was hooked. But convincing himself it was
a worthy vocation was no easy feat.

A Practical Degree

I took to painting, but it never occurred to me that I could pursue it professionally.
I was going to be an engineer: my father was in the hardware business, my
mother's family was in construction, and as a child I spent my time with Tinkertoy
and Meccano sets. I liked the look of bridges and structures. My marks in school
suggested I had a certain aptitude, so I enrolled in the engineering program at
Memorial University.

Though I ended up only taking one year of pre-engineering, two things
I learned there still serve me to this day. First off, I learned the fundamentals
of perspective. Secondly, I learned how to survey. The surveying we did was
basic triangulation — no satellites, lasers, or anything like that — with a
transit and a level. It not only gave me a sense of measurement and inspired

me to see the environment in a new way but also provided me with a trade for summer employment. At that time, if you could run a level, you had no problem getting a job.

Unfortunately, I ended up failing a lot of my classes. I had to consider other options. One fall, a couple of buddies decided they were going off to Mount Allison University in New Brunswick. My mother always wanted me to be a doctor, so I used the pre-med program at Mount Allison as an excuse to go away with them.

I had no intention of enrolling in the school's fine arts department, but I thought I could drop by every so often, stand on the side, and receive some instruction. By that point, I had my own watercolours to take along. When I arrived, I showed them to the professors in the department — including Lawren Harris and Alex Colville — and they were immediately enthusiastic. Lawren Harris even wrote my father, suggesting I switch from pre-med to fine arts.

After a year of pre-med, I couldn't stop thinking about painting. The idea of being an artist was growing on me, but I was too scared to go all the way. Instead, I switched into a general arts program.

The effect of being around the department was still huge. At the time, the world was entering the heyday of abstract expressionism. Interior decorators were buying up these big, brash paintings for penthouses because they were seen as "muscly" and "American." In the midst of this movement came Alex Colville, a man with three or four children, who wore a proper suit, walked to church on Sunday, lived in a nice little house, and was nonetheless a credible artist. The evidence of his combination of small-town decency and mainstream respect was very important for me.

The Grand Tour

After a year and a half at Mount Allison, I quit school cold turkey. My girlfriend, Mary, and I had been put in charge of decorating the junior prom. I worked all fall designing murals for the gymnasium and enjoyed it so much that I didn't go to any classes. In no shape to write the Christmas exams, I quit. I came back to St. John's, set up a studio in my bedroom, and started to paint full-time. I found I could sell watercolours for about $35 a pop, which put some money in my pocket — and kept me out of my father's pocket.

My father suggested that, if I was going to do this as a career, I should probably go to art school. I decided to take a trip and see what was being offered. I flew to New York to check out all the top colleges — what we used to call the "Art School League." Unfortunately, the students were on holidays and there were no professors to talk to me. I wandered around New York with no idea how dangerous the city was at the time. I walked into Abercrombie and Fitch to see what kind of fishing tackle they had. I then went to the Metropolitan Museum, the Whitney Museum, and the Museum of Modern Art. I sought out works for which I already had references. I wanted to see a Winslow Homer, a Picasso, and a Paul Klee in the flesh. What impressed me most was that this stuff was real. It wasn't "entertainment": this wasn't something rich dilettantes did to while away the hours or something crazy bohemians did because they didn't want to do real work. I recognized that this was an important, authentic, and meaningful line of work, a legitimate pursuit for a career. In many ways, it was essential to humanity.

When it was all done, I returned to Newfoundland and took up my brushes again. Soon, Mary and I got married and I found a job surveying runways and laying out buildings for a construction company that worked for an American naval base. Because I was given a weekly wage, I'm able to tell people it was the only real job I ever had. I started living in a small cabin my family had built near the site. I was there alone without electricity, but it was incredibly important for my early development as a painter.

Glasgow

When it came time to pick an art school, I decided I didn't want to be in New York or Toronto. Instead, I opted to go to Great Britain. I knew there were good schools there and it was close to Continental Europe. I went to the library, found the names and addresses of British schools, and wrote off to a few of them. I didn't even send a portfolio. I just described my background. The most favourable response came from the Glasgow School of Art, and even though I didn't know much about it, I accepted the offer. It was only later, when I looked into it, that I discovered how well reputed the school was.

For the two years I spent in Glasgow, we never had a single painting class. It was all drawing, sculpture, and design. It was a wonderful experience, but very academic. In the end, I didn't complete the course. For personal reasons, I decided to return to Mount Allison and finish a fine arts degree there. Mary's father was in New Brunswick and he was quite elderly. Furthermore, we had a child by this point and I didn't know how the hell I was going to make a living. I knew I couldn't live off my father for the rest of my life. I figured I'd wind up teaching or designing posters for the tourism board. I really had no idea — how was I supposed to?

I knew that I didn't want to live in a city. "If I'm going to live east of the Restigouche," I said to myself, "I'm better off at Mount Allison." That way, if a job opened up at a regional high school or something, I'd know about it. A degree from Mount Allison would also be more important in that environment than a leaving certificate from the Glasgow School of Art.

When we got to Mount Allison, all the old professors treated me as if I were a fellow professional. I hardly ever went to class. I worked at home and brought my art in to school when I'd finished. They would give it a mark and slot it into some course I was supposedly taking.

Life as a Curator

In 1961, Memorial University wanted to extend its departments. I was hired to set up and arrange art classes, which had never been offered before. Lo and behold, in the basement of the new art library I found a room that had been set aside as a gallery. Joe Smallwood, Premier of Newfoundland, had promised the local arts club that he would build them a gallery and,

Christopher Pratt: "When opportunity knocked, I was home."

apparently, this was it. But the university decided to take it over and expand it. All of a sudden, I wound up becoming the first curator of the Art Gallery of Newfoundland and Labrador. Though it may have been the last thing I expected, the job offered security and — now with two kids — I decided to take it.

The gallery put on a few shows, but I got miserable. I suffered from gastrointestinal distress. I was sure I was dying, though the doctor assured me I was not. I finally cracked. It got to the point where I hated every concrete block in that building and every frigging muffin in the cafeteria. My cabin burnt down and my father purchased a place in Salmonier. I asked if I could live on the property and keep it heated in the winter. "It's about time," my father said. "I knew you wanted to paint pictures. It's clear you don't want to be a teacher."

Painting, Full-Time

Gradually, I began taking an interest in silkscreen work. I recognized that the way we had been taught screen print at Mount Allison — with a wooden frame hinged on a piece of plywood, some glue, and some lacquer — was the basic form of printmaking. I could do it in Salmonier and sell my work to survive. With silkscreening, I found real artistic credibility — plus it could also pay for Christmas.

When I talk to students, I remind them that things went for me as they'll never go for anybody else. I had a number of opportunities, and when opportunity knocked, I was home. I was always making stuff, not just thinking about it and staring into my belly button.

When I was at Mount Allison, I had done a print called *Boat in Sand* and shown it to Alex Colville. Russell Harper, the curator of the National Gallery of Canada, came through Sackville, saw this print, and the next thing I knew, it got into the biennial at the gallery. Then they purchased it. I was still a student, but I had paintings in successive biennials. When I came to Salmonier, I already had a demonstrable market for my work, as well as letters from a number of dealers inquiring about my paintings. I sent off my first few watercolours and silkscreens, and soon I had a dealer in New Brunswick and one in Newfoundland. Toronto came soon after. In 1969, while travelling around the country with the Canada Council, I met Mira Godard, who had a gallery on Sherbrooke Street in Montreal. She came to Newfoundland to see my studio and eventually put on a show of my work in Montreal.

There were times — especially when I was in Glasgow and when I was able to travel with the Canada Council — when I realized the "provincial" aspect of what I was doing. I recognized the limitations of confining myself to an environment like the Maritimes. I was never able to have knock 'em dead conversations with other painters. There have been points when I have had ideas for particular kinds of work — either sketches or notes — and dismissed them, thinking they did not constitute "real art." Then, travelling across Canada, I would see people doing exactly what I'd

I think it's important for young artists to see the original versions of major works of art. You need to go to cities like New York, Florence, and Paris. Seeing actual art is far more important than seeing other artists. That difference is one I'd like to emphatically underline. I never wanted to live in a so-called artistic community. The only time I tried to, I didn't enjoy it and felt it was something an artist should always avoid.

— Alex Colville, celebrated artist whose paintings have appeared everywhere from the National Galley of Canada to London's Tate Museum considered. Moments like that, you realize that the great advantage of being in a group is that you get a sense of expansiveness that you don't necessarily feel in a small place like Salmonier, especially when you're on your own.

Mira Godard, who eventually became my dealer, never put any pressure on me. Still, there were times when she told me, very gently, that she felt I had a lot of creative ability that could not be resolved in my environment. It may have been conservatism or cowardice — either way, I spent my career in Newfoundland.

"I feel very strongly that getting out and about — different places, different jobs — gives you a sense of what you might want to do later on."

Though hailing from the cold streets of Toronto, **John Godfrey** always dreamed of Europe. His mother was intrigued by the wave of colourful immigrants arriving from Europe following the Second World War and transformed the Godfrey home into the centre of an émigrés community. "My biggest wish was to be reborn as a Hungarian count," says Godfrey, "penniless but stylish."

His father, a lawyer, man about town, and big supporter of the Liberal Party of Canada, pushed Godfrey towards politics, though never too hard. Education was always important, a maxim Godfrey still vouches for, having spent two and a half decades in and around universities. At thirty-four, he became the youngest university president in Canada at King's College in his adopted home of Halifax. Then, after publishing his doctoral thesis and editing the *Financial Post* (now reborn as the *National Post*) for five years, he ran as the Liberal candidate in the federal riding of Don Valley West in Toronto in 1993 and won. In 2003, he entered Paul Martin's cabinet as minister of state for infrastructure and communities, where he undertook the vital portfolio of representing Canada's cities.

The Lessons of the 1960s

During my undergraduate period — 1961 to 1965 — both the free speech movement at Berkeley and the civil rights movement in Alabama were in full swing, and they began to have spillover effects in Canada. One day stands out in my memory as a turning point: November 22, 1963. The night before, there had been a debate at Hart House between students from the University of Toronto and Ontario Premier John Robarts. The next morning, many of the same students turned up for the first demonstration in which I had ever taken part. It involved a peaceful march over to Queen's Park to ask — it sounds sweet when I think about it now — for the premiers to be *nice* to Quebec at a forthcoming federal-provincial conference. Then, as we drifted back to the buttery at Trinity College, the news came through from Dallas: John F. Kennedy had just been shot.

Somehow those moments will always be connected in my mind, from the good old-fashioned debating society to the turning of the whole political culture associated with Kennedy's assassination — a twenty-four-hour pivot point in my life and consciousness.

Student demonstrations became increasingly frequent. They were part of the "new style" of politics, which was like adding another radio band. If AM is traditional politics — nominations, parties, and that kind of thing — FM is extra-traditional, including protests, demonstrations, and group action.

I think my sensitivity to the new style has been very useful. Though the techniques change, they rely on the same forces. Outside the political system, the key elements are always based on surprise and raising people's awareness. Nowadays, I am neither terrified nor puzzled by the FM band because I once belonged to it. In fact, what strikes me most is how much less of it there is.

Summer Experiments

I was quite systematic in choosing where I would work after each year of university. If during one summer I worked somewhere in Canada, I would try to work abroad for the next. This gave me a variety of experiences. The summer is a great time to experiment and try new things. I feel very strongly that getting out and about — different places, different jobs — gives you a sense of what you might want to do later on.

The first summer, I went to the Rockies without knowing very much. Calgary was going through one of its boom phases and I managed to hook up with this oil company as a member of a seven-person crew. There were three geologists, a helicopter pilot, a mechanic, a cook, and the assistant cook, which was me. It was an inverted social pyramid and I was at the bottom. Everyone looked down on me, even the cook.

John Godfrey: "The simple willingness to be interested in other societies is a key to many jobs."

The next year, I got to work in London, England, for the research department of Wood Gundy. I wish I could say that I got the position by virtue of being a hard-working fellow, but it was really thanks to a family connection. Though it was fun for a summer, working for a big investment bank certainly disabused me of the notion that I would want to do it full-time.

A Simple Willingness

I also spent a summer at an insurance company in Lévis, Quebec. I lived in a boarding house and worked in town. One night, while the Royal Commission on Bilingualism and Biculturalism was holding a public hearing, I went to dine in Quebec City with a young lawyer friend of mine who picked me up in a flashy sports car. After dinner, when I got out at the hearing, I managed to hitch the bottom of my pants to his door and there was a corresponding rip on my bottom. I had to enter the hall with great dignity — and an umbrella covering my posterior!

The meeting itself had been taken over by *souverainistes*, and anyone who tried to speak in English was hooted down. I remember an old lady stood up to talk. "Life is a mystery," she began. Then everyone started yelling, "*Parlez français, parlez français!*"

I decided to get up and, in my awkward way, address the audience. "I hadn't realized we were here to discuss separation," I said. "I thought we were here to discuss the future of the country." They actually listened and respected what I had to say. The reason was that I said it all in French.

As nervous as I may have been, particularly because of the rip in my pants, I learned that if you make the effort people cannot reasonably attack you. It meant having enough respect to learn somebody else's language. It's a life lesson that I've applied to politics. I've always tried to understand the cultures and languages of the people I represent, whether they're from Estonia or Sri Lanka, and to have some appreciation of their specific culture: in general, to be more empathetic to people, to have a feeling of where they're from, what it is they read, and what their values are. The simple willingness to be interested in other societies is a key to so many jobs. You become more at ease in the world because you know what kinds of questions to ask.

Going to Oxford

In my twenties, I had a very simple equation: time versus money. It seemed that either I could go into some high-paying profession where, if I wanted more money, I had to work harder or be prepared to accept a lower standard of living and be paid, essentially, in time. The great virtue of the academic profession was that you had more freedom, spent your time reading and talking about books, and were always surrounded by young people. The activities were fundamentally pleasant.

My father was very supportive of my choice. He never believed in nepotism, and while he would have been happy had I gone into law, under his standards, I would not have been able to be hired by his firm. He always imagined two scenarios: that I wouldn't be good enough — which didn't really bother him — or that I would be good and end up working for a rival firm. Regardless, I viewed law as I did curling: it was something in which I had no interest but might want to take up when I was older.

I decided to continue my education — and indulge my love for Europe — by going to Oxford for a master's in history. While there, I studied European history generally and developed a focus on France, gradually moving out of social and religious history and into economic and military history. My doctoral thesis was on France in the First World War.

Since I didn't have any grants, I initially went to Oxford on a "daddy-ship." Once I began my doctoral program, however, I got a Canada Council Doctoral Fellowship which, given the exchange rate and the relatively low fees being charged, made me quite a prosperous fellow. On top of that, I got junior fellowship money from Oxford. Though there were no funds going into my savings account, I became quite self-sufficient, with some money left over to travel. I was being paid in time.

Value Added

I would be the first to admit that I was never a fantastic scholar. I could not see myself producing great academic oeuvres for the rest of my life. I did my bit, conducting research and eventually getting my thesis published. But I didn't think the world needed me as a professional historian.

I often thought about politics. My father gave me only one piece of advice. "Don't do it too soon," he said. "You can get involved, but don't think about running until you've actually had a career in something else."

He was right. Politicians fall into two categories. There's the professional class — people like Jean Chrétien and Sheila Copps — who started out in politics, either as a municipal councillor or a staffer and moved up. They have great virtues because of their street smarts. They understand the game. But because they don't bring an outside perspective, they are rarely able to shake up the system. Adding value to politics requires more than simply being an efficient minister or member of Parliament — that's just table stakes; it gets you into the game. Making sure the mail gets answered and the trains run on time accounts for 80 percent. The other 20 percent is the value added, where you can really claim to be part of an effort to change things. This is more likely to happen if you're not a complete professional politician, if you're aware of the outside world and can bring something in to improve the general state of things.

Back in Canada

I'd also made a decision, after having lived outside of Canada for some time, that if I wanted to make a difference, I couldn't do it as a stranger in another country. I had to be a citizen and a participant. At Oxford, I was very careful about limiting my participation in demonstrations. It would have been irresponsible. I wasn't a citizen, so if I walked away, I wouldn't have to live with the consequences of my actions. Therefore, I denied myself the privilege of fully engaging in the political life of Great Britain.

If I was ever going to make things happen, I would have to, by definition, do it in Canada. At first, I developed a plan where I would be an "internal foreign service officer," living in different parts of the country four years at a time, but, like so many other things in life, it didn't work out that way. Though maybe a good idea, it wasn't practical.

I came back when I was twenty-seven. It was December 1969 and I was supposed to finish my thesis in the summer of 1970, but it took longer than expected. Instead, I began looking at ads for academic positions. There were two jobs available to teach modern French history, one at Dalhousie and one at Carleton. I interviewed for both and, after getting the first offer from Dalhousie, did what any good negotiator would do by firing back

Coming out of university, I worked in advertising while shooting short films on the side. I was never prepared to focus on one at the expense of the other. It became possible for me to shift entirely into making films, but I didn't want to live in a one-room apartment and eat off a hot plate for the rest of my life. My art was the food that nourished me, not something for which I needed to starve.

If I were to give advice to a young filmmaker, it's as simple as this: don't blend in with all the other would-be directors who go to film school and shoot arty shorts that nobody wants to watch. There's nothing wrong with starting from a commercial perspective.

—**Barry Avrich**, president of Echo Advertising and director of 2005's *The Last Mogul* a cable to the history department at Carleton saying, "Look, I've had an offer. Where do I stand with you?" They were very straightforward, saying they were going to take more time. In the end, it worked out well because my intuition had pointed me to Dalhousie anyway. Halifax had a more attractive campus, and besides, it seemed more European.

I was hired as a full-time assistant professor. It was a great set-up: I started renting a bachelor apartment down on Barrington Street and got myself a bicycle. Besides, it was wonderful to be teaching in my late twenties because I wasn't that removed from my students.

The Road to the Presidency

Because I never cooked, I eventually started eating at the cafeteria at King's College. I also joined some wild student societies, ultimately becoming head of the literary and debating societies. The next year, when King's was choosing its don of residence, I applied and, because I had become quite involved with the college, got the position.

I was don for five years while living in residence. It was a grand old time. Then, when I was away on sabbatical, there was a "coup" and I became a contender for the college presidency. It was a good policy to be in exile, far removed from all the rumbles that were going on. I came back at Christmas, and the vice-president of the day, a colleague of mine from the history department, said, "John, you may not know it, but there's been a bit of difficulty here. In the event of the president feeling unable to continue, would you be available?"

"You bet!" I said.

"Well, that's good," he added, ever the English historian. "Because if you're going to kill the king, it's as well to have a prince handy!"

"I never followed a roadmap..."

While most are content to hunker down in one industry for the majority of their careers, **Phyllis Yaffe**, the CEO of Alliance Atlantis Communications, has skipped from books to magazines to television. Before being corralled by Alliance Atlantis to jumpstart its new specialty channel, Showcase, in 1995, Yaffe had served as director of the Canadian Children's Book Centre, vice-president of marketing for Owl Communications, and chair of what is now the Harold Greenberg Fund. The unifying thread through these career shifts? A sincere and unflappable love of Canadian culture.

A literature major who cheered on Tommy Douglas in her high school days, Phyllis Yaffe is perhaps the only former librarian to become the CEO of a major international media company. After watching her father toil away at a job he despised, the Winnipeg native vowed to find a career that made her happy. She would never have guessed it would lead to the top of a corporate office tower.

No Career Waiting at the Other End

I was always jealous of people who had epiphanies and said things like, "Oh, I want to be a tuba player for the rest of my life!" I never had that moment. I just fell into my first job, which led to the next job, which led to the next. It would be wrong to assume everything happened by luck, but I never set out to have a particular kind of career.

I took English literature at the University of Manitoba. It was clear when I finished that no career was waiting for me at the other end. By the time I graduated, I had a better idea of what I didn't want than what I actually wanted to be. I knew I could probably be a teacher, but I didn't want that. I didn't want to be in business either. It was the 1960s and we were all Tommy Douglas supporters: business was the enemy. You could be a doctor, a forest ranger, or a hippie, just as long as you didn't go into business.

The Library

Everyone seemed to be travelling to Europe. That was just what they did. They weren't interested in one specific country, just "Europe" in general. As someone who had never been outside of North America, I was itching to join the exodus. After graduating, I planned to get a summer job that would earn me enough money to go. I hadn't really thought beyond that. I just thought travelling would be fantastic.

When I asked my father where I should go for a summer job, he said, "Go to City Hall." So that's what I did. I didn't ask why, I just went. The next morning, I walked into City Hall and went up to the personnel counter. "I'm here to see what kind of jobs you have for people with BAs," I said. The woman behind the counter pulled out a piece of paper and scrolled down a long list. "Ah, BAs," she said, near the bottom. "The library is hiring BAs."

I'd never considered being a librarian before. Not even for a second. But the library was two blocks away, so I strolled over and had an interview. When the woman asked me which section I'd like to work in, I opened my mouth and, mysteriously, "Children" came out. "Perfect," she said. "We need someone to work on the bookmobile."

The bookmobile was a metal trailer full of books that stationed itself in neighbourhoods that didn't have libraries. Since this was Winnipeg, the trailer was freezing cold in the winter and boiling hot in the summer. But I loved it. Kids would come in and I'd get to tell them what to read. Then they'd come back and ask for more. They were like sponges, soaking up every page.

I also worked behind the reference desk at a library. People would phone in with research inquiries, asking questions like, "Can you find out what the three longest rivers in Africa are?" We'd say, "Sure," and then get to work, poring through thousands of books. We were like Google. We had to know exactly what reference materials were in each book. Every inquiry was a new puzzle. I loved everything about it.

Going Pro

By the end of the summer, I was having so much fun that I didn't go to Europe. I stayed at that job for two full years. My official job title at the Winnipeg Public Library was "Library Assistant," but they used to call the position "BA." I realized I couldn't be a "BA" forever. I decided I wanted to become a professional librarian, so I enrolled at the University of Alberta to get a degree in library science.

I was interested in becoming a children's librarian. For my degree, I took a lot of courses in children's literature and public libraries. I was interested in getting people to read books. I'd grab the new books when they came into the libraries and read them before anyone else. Then people would come in and ask about what to read. I'd recommend one of the recent titles. "If you liked this kind of book before," I'd say, "you might like this new one."

When I finished my degree, I came back and worked as a children's librarian for one year. When my husband moved to Toronto for his PhD, I got a job as a reference librarian at Seneca College. There, my responsibilities were slightly different. Students would come in and outline what their project topics were and I'd help them find what they needed.

Being a librarian — whether it was working with children or doing research-focused work — was amazing training. I was learning how to find information, how to be thorough, and how to learn.

Emergency Librarian

The 1970s — it was a time in society when big questions got asked about our values. Some of my fellow librarians and I felt our functions were essential to society. We believed that people's lives could be improved if they had more information at their fingertips. In 1973, some colleagues and I started a magazine called *Emergency Librarian*. It was a professional feminist magazine for librarians in Canada — the ultimate niche market. It was about empowering people: empowering librarians and their patrons. It was about getting information to librarians and their readers. It was about how 90 percent of the librarian population was female but all the chief librarians were male. We tried to call it *Liberated Librarian*, but there was already a magazine with that name. So we settled on *Emergency Librarian*.

I was going to take on the world. I was going to be a children's librarian who brought reading to kids. I became the union steward at Seneca College. I served both the faculty and the librarians, because we were in the same union. I was completely committed to my mission. But then something happened.

The Canadian Children's Book Centre

Irma McDonough, a librarian at the provincial library service, was trying to start up a Canadian children's book centre. Many countries had them. Canadians didn't know that they had children's books written by Canadians. Irma was a huge fan of *Emergency Librarian*. We met and chatted and I began writing book reviews for her. Eventually, she asked me to come on board as the centre's director. I knew all the books and the cause appealed to me. I thought I'd do the job for a year and then come back to the library, but when I asked my dean for a leave of absence, he refused. I had to decide: should I stay or should I go? In the end, I couldn't pass up the opportunity.

It was a tough job. Only about fifty Canadian children's books were being published a year and most people didn't think they were very good. "They're not good quality, they're not well edited, and the covers are no good," people would say. But around that time Dennis Lee wrote *Alligator Pie* and Mordecai Richler wrote *Jacob Two-Two Meets the Hooded Fang*. They were big successes and a number of others followed soon thereafter. The library world was suddenly keen to have Canadian books on the shelves, but the marketing push to get the public excited was difficult. I did a lot of media tours across the country, talking about why people should read Canadian books to their kids. It wasn't easy to start, but thanks to the Canadian and Ontario Arts Councils, we had the money to finance the program.

Jobs Leading to Jobs Leading to Jobs...

Originally, I thought I'd go back to library work, but I never did. After the book centre gig, I went to work for the Association of Canadian Publishers (ACP). The community of organizations in the Canadian book scene was quite small, so everyone knew everyone. The ACP needed a director, they asked me, and I said yes. It was different from my previous job because it was far more political. I essentially became a lobbyist.

In 1970, Ryerson Press, the founding textbook publisher in Canada, was sold to McGraw-Hill from the United States. That got people worried about the future of Canadian publishing. By the time I arrived, the momentum was turning and people were basically saying, "You have to stop the Americans from buying us out, or we'll lose all of Canadian publishing."

Running the ACP was a heady thing, because it was such an exciting time in Canadian politics. The issues we were fighting for were at the top of the federal government agenda — cultural nationalism and business development — so everything you did had a certain intensity.

When I started, I was scared to death that people would ask me questions I couldn't answer. I had my secretary answer the phone for me and tell me who was calling so I could prepare what to say before picking up. By the time I left the association five years later, nothing could happen in the Canadian book publishing industry that I didn't know about. I was at the heart of the industry, at least the Canadian-owned industry.

It was very hard to leave. It had been exciting and we'd been successful, but enough was enough. By then, it was never a question of going back to a library. My time as a librarian taught me to think and organize myself. It was a big part of my later success, but I couldn't have gone back. Besides, by the time I left the ACP, libraries had changed.

Starting from Scratch, Again

I needed a new challenge. Through my work with the ACP, I had become very good friends with Annabel Slaight, one of the co-founders of *Owl* magazine, a popular science and nature magazine for kids. She wanted me to come and do marketing for the magazine. We joke about this now, but I had no idea what marketing was. She said, "Don't worry. Come and we'll figure it out." So I did. In the end, though, it was only part-time work.

Peter Grant, the external counsel at the ACP, was working with First Choice Communications, the pay-TV company, as they established what they now call the Harold Greenberg Fund. The fund was set up to help finance Canadian film projects. Peter was looking for someone to run the fund and he approached me. The opportunity was very exciting. And because I loved working at *Owl* part-time, I figured I could do both. I asked Annabel and she seemed fine with the idea, so for the next eight years, I worked at *Owl* in the morning and at the fund in the afternoon.

Moving from books to magazines and then to television and film was challenging. Like every other time I've moved into a new area, I had to learn from scratch. But, in a way, working in Canadian cultural industries is similar across the board. They all require political will to exist.

I was very lucky. Not many people are ever in the position to change industries like that. All I ever did was find things that I liked and believed in. I never followed a roadmap and I never cared about the money beyond what I needed to live. I was passionate about Canadian culture and getting Canadian works into people's hands. Because I was passionate, I worked hard. Because I worked hard, people noticed. And then there must have been a little luck involved too.

*"How could I call myself a sociologist if all I had
done was hang around other academics?"*

Angus Reid created the largest market research company in Canada, the Angus Reid Group, used by governments and corporations for everything from election polls to consumer studies. Though the company started above a Winnipeg 7-Eleven, Reid hit the big time when Liberal leadership candidate John Turner made him his official pollster in 1984. "I was very pushy," Reid recalls. "Turner needed a pollster, so I asked for the job. If you don't ask, you'll never get anywhere." In 2000, Reid sold his company to Paris-based Ipsos for $100 million and has since gone on to serve as CEO for both Vision Critical and Angus Reid Strategies. He is also the author of *Shakedown: How the New Economy Is Changing Our Lives* (1996).

His star was not always so bright. Angus Reid was one of eight children. Throughout high school, he worked as a janitor and carry-out boy at his local Safeway store in Regina. A strong student in math and chemistry, he planned to study engineering at university, but after failing Grade 12 English he was forced to stay on at the Safeway for another year. After his friends left for university, Reid began to consider why certain people became more successful than others. Questions of history, economic influence, and personal biography began to intrigue him. Ultimately, Reid opted to apply for a general arts program.

University: Second Time Lucky

The extra year I spent stocking shelves made me hungry for success. I had just met Margaret, the woman I'd eventually marry, and I remember looking at myself and saying, "Here I am, a high school dropout working at Safeway. Boy, I sure don't want to do this for the rest of my life."

When I arrived at the University of Manitoba, I was overwhelmed

Angus Reid: "I don't really like being a student."

with the exciting new opportunities to learn. I found most of my high school subjects boring. Suddenly, I could study wonderful things like economics, sociology, and political science in courses that analyzed the way the world worked. I wanted to soak up as much as I could.

I remember the first sociology class I ever took. I had a professor named Brian Finnegan. I had never done well in any high school course that required me to write, but as Professor Finnegan was handing back our first papers, he walked up to me and smiled. "You got an A+," he said. I felt as though there was finally something I was good at.

Moving Forward

It was a bit of a coin toss over whether I should go into economics or sociology, but sociology won out. I'm not sure I would encourage anyone to go into the field today, but this was the late 1960s. There was a palpable and pervasive sense that we could create a better world. We had just had Lyndon Johnson's Great Society and people believed that if we could understand how societies worked, then we could tinker around and improve them. Sociology sought to understand populations by doing hard survey research. The subject had yet to be polluted by crazy Marxists.

The summer after my first year, I was energized like I'd never been before. I had three jobs. I sold paintbrushes door to door, worked for the Canadian Pacific Railway, and drove a taxi. The CPR had added a second train to the system, so we worked from either 8:00 a.m. to 4:00 p.m. or 4:00 p.m. to midnight. I felt like that wasn't enough to keep me busy, so I drove a cab in the off hours. Later in the summer, I picked up the door-to-door sales job for extra money.

I was a very excited student. In my second year, I made sociology my major. I never thought about where it would take me when I finished, but I didn't care.

Graduate Studies

I had a stroke of luck. With the baby boom pouring into universities in the late 1960s, there was a teacher shortage. In my third year, I was given a job as a teacher's assistant. Suddenly, I was earning $500 for teaching a first-year sociology course. Better still, teaching brought me into closer touch with the rest of the department, allowing me to see what the academic life looked like.

Around that time, I decided to apply for a master's degree in sociology. In those days, it was still very rare to do graduate studies. The number of people who even went to university for an undergraduate degree was still a small percentage of the population. But I was at the leading edge of the baby boom. We saw ourselves as a "new" generation. We were determined to do things differently than our parents. Studying sociology rather than going into law or engineering was my way of declaring to the world that I was taking a big, bold step into a new age.

I squeaked into graduate studies just as I'd squeaked into university. In the third and fourth years of my undergraduate degree, I got really involved in student politics and extracurricular activities. My grades slipped down to a C+. If it had been today, and every university was looking to improve their position on the *Maclean's* rankings, I would never have gotten to do my master's. Thankfully, someone at the University of Manitoba had pity on me and thought I might be a good guy. They accepted me into the program on a conditional basis. Without that, who knows where I would have ended up?

Survey Research

Only when I began my master's did I latch on to survey research and polling. Shortly after arriving in the program, I met a visiting American professor who had a grant to do a community survey on health and housing in Churchill, Manitoba. Because I was somewhat more mathematically inclined than many of my colleagues (and because the professor and I got along), he asked if I would be the team leader.

That was the first big survey I ever did. I analyzed the results and completed the report. I even ended up writing my thesis on that research. While most people took two years to complete their master's, I finished mine in a year. It was a terrible thesis about voluntary association membership in Churchill. I simply took the collected survey data and adapted it to fit an obscure sociological theory. All I had to do was show I could jump through the correct academic hoops.

Transitions

At that point, I needed a job. Unfortunately, I wasn't entirely sure what to do. Soon after finishing, I met David Fish, a sociologist teaching at the university's faculty of medicine. The federal government had sponsored him to do a major survey of dental students. I know this may sound humorous now, but the faculty had some flaky idea that if they understood dental socialization, they could pick the right people to be dentists in rural areas. I didn't care about any of that shit. To me, it was just a job. I was twenty-two years old and working on a national survey.

In the meantime, I applied for a Canada Council Doctoral Fellowship and got accepted to Carleton University. The University of Manitoba had been a practical and down-to-earth place; it was hardly an intellectual powerhouse. Carleton, on the other hand, was more of a "big thinker" institution. They had more students going into sociological theory, phenomenology, and the philosophy of science. When I arrived, I had to quickly adjust to the environment and the approach.

It was intellectually challenging, but I did everything I could to get through the program as quickly as possible. I don't really like being a student. One of the guys from the dental study committee ended up being my thesis advisor. He was a very practical sociologist named Bruce McFarlane. As had been the case for my master's, I was shamelessly pragmatic. "Aha!" I said. "I've got a data set here based on a national study of dental students. I could use this data to write my dissertation. Then I can get out into the world and earn a living." That's precisely what I did. I finished my doctorate in two and a half years.

By that time, it was clear I didn't really mesh with academic sociology. Nevertheless, a good friend encouraged me to apply for a National Research Scholar Award, which the government was offering to recent PhD graduates, funding the first five years of their careers. I knew I didn't love the academic life, but something made me apply anyway.

When I got the award, I entered what I call the "lost years" of my career. For five years, I was an academic at the University of Manitoba — an assistant and then an associate professor with tenure, funded by the feds. I was bored out of my skull. Everything at university works at a glacial pace. You have something you want to study, but you spend a year writing proposals and another two waiting for a response.

In 1976–77, I wrote a proposal for a study on the impact of a new system for funding Medicare in Canada. I thought it was a strategic and necessary investigation that cut straight to the heart of the larger issue of health financing. They looked at the proposal and said, "This is really good. We encourage you to reapply. We'll come back to it in six months." I thought that was bullshit. Besides, who wants to spend their life writing journal articles for a bunch of other academics to read?

Around that time I read John Kenneth Galbraith's autobiography, *A Life in Our Time.* Here was a guy who moved back and forth between academia and the world of action. He was writing papers one moment and advising American presidents the next. That really inspired me. How could I call myself a sociologist if all I had done was hang around other academics?

Starting a Business

During the late 1970s, I did a bit of preliminary work for a number of political candidates in the area. There was a federal election looming on the horizon and people asked if I could check the waters. I did most of that work as personal favours. None of my work had been publicly reported, but Lloyd Axworthy must have caught word of it. Lloyd had taught in Manitoba and, until recently, had been the lone Liberal in the provincial legislature. The Liberal Party had Martin Goldfarb, a big Toronto pollster, do a survey in the riding of Winnipeg South to see if Axworthy would have a chance against the independent candidate running against him. *Maclean's* had recently named Goldfarb Canada's most influential citizen. His survey suggested that Axworthy didn't have a prayer.

One day David Walker, Lloyd's campaign president, arrived at my door asking for a second opinion. I looked at Goldfarb's survey results and asked some people about the methodology he had used. A significant sampling flaw in his work had produced an over-representation of Conservative voters. "This is a bunch of horseshit!" I said.

When I mentioned the flaws to Goldfarb, he said, "Listen, kid. Leave it up to us guys in Toronto. We know what we're doing." That was the wrong thing to say to me at the time.

When my husband and I were building our winery, I thought we were making a mistake by investing everything in the business. We had to mortgage our home. I'm a person who needs safety and security: I don't want to risk losing what I have. That was the scariest time of my life. Luckily, in the end, it turned out to be the right move.

That's why my pet peeve is the term "entrepreneur." A lot of people say they're entrepreneurs, but many were handed something from a spouse or a parent. They don't know what it's like to have nothing, to not know how to balance the next payment and to risk everything for an idea. Very few people have actually done that. To me, an entrepreneur is someone who risks everything. The real entrepreneurs are the people who can't sleep because of the fear of losing everything.

— **Rossana Magnotta**, co-founder and president of Magnotta Wineries

That night, as I flew to Ottawa for a grant committee meeting, I remember thinking, "This Goldfarb's a big fancy consultant with lots of influence, but his work doesn't look that good. Why can't I do it instead?" That's when I decided to expand my consulting practice to get more involved in survey research on a commercial basis.

Eventually, I left academia and threw everything into my business. At the age of twenty-seven, I incorporated a company called CanWest Survey Research and set up shop above a 7-Eleven. I was scared out of my mind. To begin with, I knew nothing about money. If you had asked me to describe the elements of a balance sheet, I wouldn't have had a clue. I started with a personal bank loan from the Toronto Dominion Bank and was totally under-capitalized for the first ten years. On a number of occasions, I almost went bankrupt. We hit a huge recession in 1982 and interest rates suddenly shot up to 19 percent. Somehow, though, I managed to skim the treetops and avoid catching a branch. Gradually I developed a nose for the business side and built a $50-million company.

When I arrived on the marketing research scene, there was a cozy arrangement amongst various players. It wasn't very competitive at all. Since I didn't take any assumptions for granted and since I knew I could only succeed with solid work, I was forced to create a full-service research company that could do everything and do it well.

There were times I thought I'd made a huge mistake. But throughout it all, I took solace in the fact that I could always go back to academia. I knew if my business failed I wouldn't necessarily have to drive a cab.

DAVID SHORE

*"I was able to start writing because I left behind
all the other commitments in my life."*

After reading F. Lee Bailey's *The Defence Never Rests* at the age
of twelve, London, Ontario–born **David Shore**'s only dream was
to become a lawyer. Everything changed, however, once he got
into law school. After the second week, he realized that, exciting
as a courtroom may be, the study of law was rather dry. He stuck
it out, doing the bare minimum of work for three years until, at the
age of twenty-two, he graduated with a law degree.

After five years, Shore ditched his legal career and moved
to Los Angeles to try his hand at scriptwriting. Going from comedic to dramatic material, he worked on a number of shows,
especially law-themed series like *The Practice* and *Law & Order*.
In 2003, he was requisitioned to create a procedural television
series that took place in a hospital. Basing the main character
partly on Sherlock Holmes and partly on himself, Shore came up
with *House, M.D.*, which premiered the following year. The show
has become a smash hit, winning Shore both an Emmy for Best
Writing and a Peabody Award in 2005.

The Law

I did well in school. I started as a math major at the University of Toronto and,
because of my grades, was able to transfer into law after two years. When I
first got there, I felt some nervous excitement because I was younger than most
of the other students. That feeling soon wore off. There's a saying about law
school — the first year they scare you to death, the second year they work you to
death, and the third year they bore you to death — but I was bored right from
the start.

I devised a plan to get by. Although I attended every single class, I would
never do the required readings. I spent fourteen hours a week in lectures and
did nothing else. In first year, I felt a little guilty, but by second year, it became a

conscious decision. Rather than fooling myself by saying I'd catch up with my readings later, I just admitted that, no, I wasn't actually going to read anything. If they failed me, they failed me. I could live with that. If they passed me, then it wasn't a bad way to spend the next two years.

Even after graduating, I knew very little about the practice of law. I still had an F. Lee Bailey vision. The articling process taught me a lot and I came to enjoy practising, certainly more than I had enjoyed law school. I articled back in London at a firm that put me in a rotation system. I got two months' exposure to many different fields. After a while, I moved to Toronto and worked for a few years at another firm, where I got bigger files. I was the young guy everybody kind of liked, which was great: whenever something new came in, they would pass it on to me, which forced me to have a fairly broad area of expertise.

I was not miserable practising law. There was obviously something missing, but I never felt I couldn't stand what I was doing. It interested me for a while, so I thought I should keep it up. Sometimes, those who have more "creative" professions believe that lawyers are simple mechanics, hammering nails into boards. That's not true. There are countless skills required to draft a contract. You have to answer all the "what-ifs." Every lawyer is going to come at a contract from a different perspective and cover the territory slightly differently. I was annoyed by people who thought we were executing a dry task.

Writing Comedy

Through my early twenties, the only writing I ever did was for the law school's monthly paper. It was a comedy rag and we wrote satirical stories. Though I never saw it as part of my future, I eventually became the co-editor. It was my only experience before coming to Los Angeles. In retrospect, I probably should have tried to write more, to see if I was any good.

While I was working in Toronto, I decided to do some stand-up comedy. I thought I was kind of funny — though people kept telling me I wasn't *that* funny. It was just observational stuff. My main influence was Jerry Seinfeld, who was starting around the same time. I had seen him on stage, even before he got his own show. He just went up and talked. He didn't hide behind voices or gimmicks. I tried to do the same thing and got a decent response: there were some laughs.

But I kept comedy on the back burner. I didn't tell many people about my stand-up gigs. My family and friends only came to my first performance. I soon stopped doing shows entirely and, for four years, focused on practising law. I became a regular lawyer — and soon worked my way up to partner. But in the back of my mind, I was still thinking about doing something else.

After the first couple of years, I started to consider dropping everything, becoming a writer, and moving to Los Angeles. My dad, always the sensible one, talked me out of it. I stayed with the firm, but after another two years, I decided to go. This time my parents were supportive, thinking perhaps that if I was still considering the opportunity, I must be serious about it. So I saved up some money and made the move.

I was lucky to be in a position to do so. Because I didn't have a new family or a girlfriend, and because I had enough saved in the bank, there was a window of opportunity that few people at my age still had. I was free. I didn't have the "golden handcuffs" — when you can't leave because you're making a living and have responsibilities. I thought, "If I'm going to do this, I have to do it now."

Los Angeles

I said I'd give myself roughly two years. I'd go down and if I fell flat on my face, I'd come right back and practise law again. As a partner in the firm, I negotiated the right to return. If I had completely failed, five years down the road my time in Hollywood would have been a little hiccup in my legal career, an interesting story to tell people.

My plan was to write comedy and maybe do some more stand-up. So I bought a computer, rented an apartment, and sat down to work on a movie screenplay.

The process of writing was not an easy one to start. For me, it helped that I had nothing else to do and didn't know a lot of people. I would write every day, not necessarily nine to five, but I would get up in the morning, walk my dog, and sit down and write.

I spent months working on that screenplay. When I was done, I gave it to some buddies to read. They took a couple of weeks with it, and during that time I wrote a *Seinfeld* script, which I also gave to them. They said, "You know the thing that took you two weeks to write? It's about as good as the thing you spent six months on." Apparently, I was better at writing for television. Also, the more I wrote, the better I got. They were right: that original script was pretty awful.

I became quite paranoid about my work. It took me a while before I started sending it out. The traditional first step was to get an agent. I didn't want to blanket every agency in town. Number one, they don't read most stuff. Number two, I was worried that they would read it, hate it, and remember my name forever. I didn't send anything until I felt comfortable with it, and I only sent to people I had connections to. I ran into a guy from university at a restaurant one night and it turned out he was an agent's assistant. So I gave him my script to pass on to another assistant, who happened to like it and eventually became my agent. He still is today.

The Way to Work

I was able to start writing because I left behind all the other commitments in my life. That's why I could never do any writing while I was working in Toronto. I kept planning to do some in my spare time, but I never did. I had to quit my job, come down to Los Angeles, and force myself to do it. By moving away from where I was, I gave myself no choice but to write. I guess I could have gone to Edmonton or something, but the great thing about Los Angeles is that I found a community of struggling writers. In Toronto, if you say you're a struggling writer, people ask, "What are you doing with the rest of your time?" In Los Angeles, "unemployed writer" is an accepted profession — and there are many others to commiserate with.

One of the ironies of the business is that you only get better by continuously writing, but you only get the opportunity to write when you're actually employed. Sitting at home and working on your own stuff isn't the same. Once you actually start writing for specific shows, it's a whole different experience.

The way it works is you write "spec scripts," which are scripts for imaginary episodes. If you write one for *Seinfeld*, it's never going to get sold to *Seinfeld*. But you show it to *Malcolm in the Middle* and hope they like your style. That's what I was doing. I wrote a lot of spec scripts for my agent to send out to show people the different styles I could do.

Getting work takes a while. It took me a year to get an agent, then another year before he got me any work. That's pretty typical. I did a freelance script for *The Untouchables*, a syndicated series, and then I was out of work again for another year. Finally, my agent set up a meeting with Paul Haggis, who was starting *Due South*. I would have been thrilled even to get a freelance job with them, but I guess they liked my stuff, so they offered to put me on staff.

Due South

The premise of *Due South* was of a Canadian Mountie who goes to Chicago to solve a crime and ends up being partnered with a hard-nosed city cop. As a writer, the pay was horrible. They hired me, expecting that I'd relocate to Toronto. I had to fight them to cover my plane ticket, which they finally bought for me. I remember that even though I wasn't getting any other work, my agent was saying, "If you want to turn this down, I support you." To hear that from your agent is a sign that you aren't doing too well financially. But I was thrilled to be employed.

It was very odd coming back to Canada. I had actually owned a home in Toronto when I was a lawyer, and I kept it for a while, renting it out, until I sold it six months before returning. The place I ended up renting was further from where we were shooting than my old house. But altogether it was a very cool experience, especially because *Due South* became such a massive hit in Canada. Afterwards, I returned to Hollywood to continue my career.

Advice

I get annoyed with people who say, "Never give up on your dreams." Not everybody is going to succeed in every single dream they have. My plan was to come to Hollywood for a couple of years, see how it went, and if I failed, go back to being a lawyer. It was a compromise I made with myself. There are so many people who don't make it in the entertainment world. If it weren't for a few lucky strokes, I could have been struggling to write in a one-bedroom apartment for the rest of my life.

There are two rules that young writers need to succeed: be obnoxious and write constantly. There's a Canadian mentality that sometimes needs to be avoided. Writers are afraid to come up to people and ask for favours. This is a business. If you want to be a doctor, you go to medical school and get a job as a doctor. It doesn't work that way in Hollywood. To a certain extent, it works because of connections. You need to get your foot in the door, which means annoying somebody into reading your stuff. There's no system here and you have to get noticed.

The second thing is writing. I never took any of the courses being offered. If you're going to succeed, it's not because somebody told you how to structure a script. You've got to find your own voice. That's the most important thing. You should be telling the story you want to tell. You don't necessarily have to write about what you know, but you need a reason for telling the story in a particular way. If some other jerk can tell the story as well as you, you shouldn't be telling it.

"It was tough to let go of the idea of being a
Bruce Cockburn or a Bob Dylan."

When **Raffi Cavoukian** was ten years old, social unrest forced his family to flee Egypt and settle in Toronto. His father, Cavouk, a professional portrait photographer, was also a gifted singer and accordion player who soon became a central figure in the city's close-knit Armenian community. The man was also strict: as a child, Raffi was forced to sing in front of family friends, and later he wasn't allowed to go on dates. The boy, however, found emancipation in the idealism of artists like the Beatles and Bob Dylan. In Grade 11, he bought a guitar for $24 at a downtown pawn shop and began playing covers of pop and folk songs.

Ten years later, Raffi recorded an album of children's songs, entitled *Singable Songs for the Very Young*. Though he had little idea at the time, Raffi had stumbled upon the ingredients for what became a cultural phenomenon. Songs like "Baby Beluga" and "Bananaphone" have since made him one of the most beloved children's performers in the world. He has recorded fourteen albums, authored twelve books, and wholly altered the way we look at entertainment for the young. In 1998, Raffi wrote *A Covenant for Honouring Children* and gave birth to a global movement he calls "Child Honouring." But Raffi's identity as a troubadour did not come easily: it involved wrenching himself free of his family's grasp and searching for his unique place in the world.

Embracing the Unknown

I realized early on that I didn't want to be in the family business. My grandfather had been a photographer, and my father followed in his footsteps. My older brother quit school to work at the studio when my father was sick and reluctantly stayed on to keep the family happy. I saw the turmoil at the heart of my father's business and didn't see a place for myself there. I wasn't sure what I would do, but I knew my interests were carrying me in a different direction.

I went to the University of Toronto with the fuzzy hope of becoming a teacher. I didn't have an innate love of teaching, but my experiences in high school had been so difficult and negative that I desperately wanted to give kids a break from the tyranny of the typical classroom. Once I arrived, things took a very different course.

New Ideas

I loved playing guitar and was well versed in the songs of Joni Mitchell, Gordon Lightfoot, and Bob Dylan, to name a few. I wanted to write and sing songs too. The late 1960s and early 1970s was a period of overwhelming social turmoil and unrest. The Vietnam War was raging and young people were looking for new ways of living. Society's old values seemed atrophied and negative. I read Martin Luther King and Mahatma Gandhi and loved their ideas of peaceful resistance. The folk music of the time spoke in a similar voice.

In my first year at university, I formed a duo with a friend and we put a few poems he'd written to music. I did some solo gigs as well, mainly playing covers. The odd time, I threw in some comedic elements like a Johnny Cash impression. Early on, I suffered from such bad stage fright that I had to drink before I went on. Gradually, though, I calmed down and began to enjoy playing in front of audiences.

Leaving Home

In the second year of university, I had an epiphany: my mind had broadened enough to see that I could leave. Integral to that psychological turning point were the writings of the Chinese sage Lao Tzu. He introduced me to the idea of paradox and yin-yang. I realized I was living in a black and white world, blind to the complexities of the universe. I needed to find out who I truly was. I needed to disregard what my parents and society wanted; I needed to find my own passion.

Up until then, I had been living with my parents. Soon after leaving home, I dropped out of university as well. I'd been spending more time in coffee shops than in class. I knew that I could keep learning about the subjects that interested me — sociology, philosophy, and religion — outside of an academic context. Leaving university was the beginning of my self-education. From that point, I focused on who I was and what I needed to learn rather than on what others were telling me.

Searching...

By selling newspapers, I scraped together enough money for rent in a communal house in Chinatown. My father pressured me to come and work in the photography studio, but I wanted nothing to do with it. I wanted to get a place of my own, grow my hair long, and write songs that would change the world. It was a naive desire, but I went with it completely.

I never used my family name, for fear that I'd get breaks because of connections and associations. I was always "Raffi," wanting to make it on my own.

Eventually, I realized I needed to do some travelling, to expand my mental horizons. I grabbed a knapsack and took off for Europe. Then, the next year, I hitchhiked across Canada, playing my guitar and doing gigs all the way. I had a wonderful time. I met people, busked my heart out, and soaked up as much of the country's character as possible.

When I came back to Toronto, I took any job I could and lived on $25 a week. I sold copies of a left-wing newspaper called *Guerrilla* on the street and worked as a guard at the university art gallery for a few weeks.

Later, I started teaching guitar lessons to make extra money. I also decided to get in touch with Deb, my high school sweetheart from whom I'd been apart for a few years. I really missed her; so I phoned and invited her to hear me play at the Oxford Inn. After the show, we talked and realized the old feelings hadn't evaporated. Within a few months, we were living together.

An Opportunity to Play

Deb's mother, Daphne, was a nursery school teacher in North Toronto. She thought her kids might like it if I sang some songs for them. I was intrigued, but I didn't know any popular children's songs — they'd never been part of my Armenian childhood. Deb and her mother had to teach me the complete lyrics to things like "Mary Had a Little Lamb."

When I went into the nursery school, I was pretty nervous. I had no idea what to expect. I parked myself on the rug with a small group of four-year-olds sitting cross-legged around me. I launched into "The More We Get Together" and a few others I had learned, including "What Should We Do with the Drunken Sailor?" — at Daphne's behest.

I came home and discussed the experience with Deb. As a primary school teacher herself, she understood that getting kids to participate was more important than whether they sang well or got the rhymes right. The conversation started me off on an earnest study of young children. I hadn't really given them any thought before that.

For the next few months, I kept singing in classrooms as part of an in-school program run by the Mariposa Folk Festival. I'd come home from my performances and tell Deb what I had learned. I'd test out everything I did in the classes in front of some of her colleagues. They helped me understand that I needed to approach the children as "whole" people. That realization was pivotal, not only for my future career, but for my emotional growth as well.

Setting Up a Label

When I was twenty-seven, I decided to set up my own record label and record an album. All the better-paying gigs went to artists with recording contracts. Other folk singers had their own labels, so I thought "why not?" It meant not having to deal with the hassle of major labels, and it meant approaching things from my own angle and at my own speed. The model appealed to me.

To secure financing, I walked into my neighbourhood bank branch and asked for a small loan. I talked to the manager and explained the importance of the project. I guaranteed that I could sell two thousand copies of the LP and pay off the loan. I can't recall if my father co-signed it, but I think I persuaded the manager based on the strength of my passion and personality.

I called the label Troubadour and recorded the songs on what became *Good Luck Boy*. I did the album layout myself on Letraset. While it didn't make my career, I sold the two thousand copies I needed to pay the bank back. That meant I was in a good position to approach them for another loan later on.

Singable Songs for the Very Young

The idea to record an album of material for children came from Deb's mother. She saw that I had a knack for applying my singing abilities to children, and she saw I was a quick learner. "You should consider making an album for the very young," she said. "As an audience, they're often neglected."

Afterwards, I went home and discussed the idea with Deb. We went out and did some "market research" to see if her mother was right. We went to stores, looked at the music in the children's bin, and saw how it was packaged: it was either too syrupy for parents to like or too dry and educational for children. None of it seemed to respect young listeners. We thought we could do it differently.

Once Deb and I made the decision, the process took over. Like with playing for adults, I needed to consider this new audience. Children have a much smaller realm of experience and a limited vocabulary. And for the songs to strike a real chord, they needed to be singable. At the same time as I tried to cater the music to young people, I was also careful not to drive parents away. I made sure that the music was pleasant to the ear.

I was very lucky. I recorded *Singable Songs for the Very Young* on an eight-track in the basement studio of Daniel Lanois's mother's home in Ancaster, Ontario. Before he went on to produce landmark albums for U2, Peter Gabriel, and Bob Dylan, Lanois was just "Dan" to us. Working with someone like Dan and co-producer Ken Whitely kept the musical quality high.

The album was a huge success, but all the sold-out shows and accolades in the world couldn't convince me to commit to being a children's entertainer. It was tough to let go of the idea of being a Bruce Cockburn or a Bob Dylan. When I sat down to record again, I decided to simultaneously release an album for adults and an album for children. By doing that, I'd bring parents over to my mature music. The plan didn't work. The adult album, *Adult Entertainment*, sold well, but the numbers at my folk music shows remained small.

Knowing how torn I was, Deb and her colleagues stressed the importance of children's music. They helped me see that my musical gifts were meant to flourish

> *After finishing my master's degree, a consulting firm recruited me and I decided to leave academia. In retrospect, I had no idea who I was. I was like a reed in the wind. I saw my colleagues jumping on the fast train to the private sector and assumed that I should get on too. Without thinking about my passions, I hopped aboard.*
>
> *I should have been more confident. I could have stayed in academia and begun crafting a career for myself, which is what I knew I wanted to do. But instead I convinced myself that I didn't want to hang around crusty academics. They weren't any fun and I didn't want to be like them.*
>
> — **Jennifer Welsh**, Oxford University Professor of International Relations and author of 2004's *At Home in the World: Canada's Global Vision for the 21st Century*

in that medium. Once I discovered that, I was able to devote myself fully to making that kind of music. I never looked back.

SURVIVORS

Canadians Who Persevered

LYNDA HAVERSTOCK

"I'm not like other people who talk about education being a right. I see it as a privilege."

It is difficult to tell that **Lynda Haverstock** — a doctor in clinical psychology, a former leader of the Saskatchewan Liberal Party, and the province's lieutenant-governor for six years — spent nearly a decade in a wheelchair, told by doctors she would never walk again.

Haverstock's path has never been an easy one. She was once a nineteen-year-old single mother. The father of the child had abandoned them, skipping town and leaving the country, never to be seen again. One of the lessons she learned throughout it all has proved invaluable: the hurdles we face define who we are and can enrich our lives.

Growing Up

I don't think my story will have much resonance with young people who have great ambition. My story is more about survival and resilience than it is about someone whose life unfolded in a more traditional way. Perhaps it will speak to a different group of people.

When I was fifteen, I had to leave school because I got pregnant. In that era, no one kept their children. Expectant teen mothers disappeared, and when they came home they didn't have children. I took a different path and decided to keep mine. My parents were tough, but they supported me. "You've made a decision to be an adult," my dad said. "From now on, that's exactly what you'll be." Since that day, he never treated me as anything but an equal.

My daughter ended up being my motivation for everything: to complete high school, to finish university, and to overcome our financial burdens. She became my focus and my purpose.

The Situation Worsens

When my daughter was about three and a half, I decided I desperately wanted to go back to school. My husband at the time was furious. "If you do," he said, "I'll leave you." I didn't think he would, because he hadn't been truthful about anything else. But he did. He left and we've never seen him since. That was thirty-eight years ago.

Pregnancy forces a mental change in girls; it forces them to grow up in a hurry. It doesn't necessarily have the same effect on men. It was hard for him to acquire the sense of obligation that I suddenly felt. It was hard for him to reconfigure his life. So he left.

The first couple of years I got three $50 child support payments. The rest of her life, there was nothing — not a phone call, not a birthday card, not a conversation, not a letter. And we didn't even know where he lived. He was somewhere in the States, probably Texas or Oklahoma.

Returning to School

I stayed on my own and never moved back home. It was hard, but I did the best I could. After returning to high school, my marks improved. I seemed to be getting my groove. I learned that education was pivotal to everything. My daughter probably could have had a better mother had I not been working and in school. But, in a way, I needed to sense that I was able to take care of her without anyone else.

I'm not like other people who talk about education being a right. I see it as a privilege. I really do, to this day. I don't think we do well by making our children see it simply as a right. All of our ancestors in Saskatchewan created tremendous legacies for us. They didn't have the financial resources or the educational background, but they had a vision and an extraordinary determination to make things happen. We live in this part of the world with access to

Being a doctoral student in engineering can be quite demanding. You have to be a marketing salesperson on one hand — when you apply for funding — and a creative researcher on the other. When I was doing my PhD, I had two children, and somewhere in the middle I went through a divorce. There were times when it was really hard. But I enjoyed my research. Every new discovery, finished paper, and award I received gave me a huge sense of accomplishment and sustained me through the frustration.

I was also motivated by the fact that I didn't want a regular nine-to-five job. I enjoyed being completely free. Academia is a great place for a single parent with two small children, because you can come home at three in the afternoon and take your kids on a "field trip" if you want to. You can also leave work early and work from home. Not many occupations allow that.

— **Indira Samarasekera**, President of the University of Alberta so many things: these are clearly privileges. If people are taught that education is a right, they'll start to take it for granted.

University

I went to the University of Saskatchewan in Saskatoon for my university degree, specializing in the education of exceptional children. It was probably the best program in Canada at the time. I was very engaged. Within two and a half years, I was given a teaching job in the department. I would learn something, apply it in practice, and then be able to teach it to others.

During the first few years, my daughter and I lived in a one-bedroom basement suite. She had to sleep in the living room. The two of us used to walk back alleys and collect pop bottles to have enough money to buy milk. When people hear that, they think, "Oh my god. How terrible. Why didn't you go on welfare?" Well, I didn't need to go on welfare. I managed to survive without it.

It was also during this time that I ended up with an unusual subset of rheumatoid arthritis. I had tremendous difficulty for about nine years. It ended up taking away my ability to walk. My twenties were challenging years in terms of work and study, both physiologically and financially. But that was the lesson. You have to understand that you're living history. You end up with retrospective knowledge. There's always a lesson that you're living through. In the end, when you look back, you see that it brought you some sort of gift. That's the real purpose of life.

Rheumatoid Arthritis

At first, I realized that I had a very odd feeling in my leg and that I was dragging my foot a bit. Then, within three or four days, I couldn't use that leg at all and my knee had ballooned. I went to the emergency room and the orthopedic surgeon told me that I must have injured myself. "You'll need surgery," he said.

The doctor had gotten it all wrong. By the time I had surgery, I was done in — because that was the last thing I should have had. I was in tremendous pain for a long time, while ninety cc's of fluid was taken out of my knee every day.

One day, I was in a hospital room and the surgeon came in with a group of students. He started telling them about my problem as if I weren't there, saying that even though I had *said* I never got injured, I was wrong. He ignored everything I had told him. Luckily, another doctor was in the room with a patient and overheard everything. The next thing I knew he took my surgeon out into the hallway and spoke with him. An hour and a half later, the new doctor, who had these long flowing grey locks, came back. "I couldn't help but overhear what you were trying to say," he said to me, as if from a vision. "I was wondering if you would allow me to do a series of tests because I think I know what might be happening."

He was right. Everything done until that point had been the reverse of what should have been done. If it weren't for that second doctor, they would have never found out what was wrong. It was then that they finally diagnosed me with a form of rheumatoid arthritis.

Hardship

I ended up with very thin legs at the top, great big knees in the middle, and complete mush on the bottom. It affected both of my legs. I was confined to a wheelchair for a year and told I'd never walk again. I had physiotherapy five days a week because I couldn't bend my legs. I couldn't even sleep with a sheet on. After that year, I moved on to arm-canes.

Lynda Haverstock: "I was confined to a wheelchair for a year and told I'd never walk again."

I was very bitter when I lost my ability to walk. In hindsight, however, it was one of the most valuable periods of my life. My mother was fantastic. There were two things she did that were so intelligent: she never moved in to help me and, within ten minutes of arriving in the house, she handed me a broom! "Isn't it grand, there's nothing wrong with your arms," she said. "You'll always be able to hold the ones you love." It was good to have her as a model.

One thing I learned was not to spend a lot of time crying over spilt milk. I had the option of feeling sorry for myself, angry and bitter. But do I want to be miserable? What kind of an option is that? Who would choose that when you only have one life to live through — or, as the case may be, push yourself through?

It was a time when I realized that you can live in grotesque pain and still have a high quality of life. What defines you is not your physical shell but your intelligence and your decency as a human being. It's impossible to predict how another person will react to you when you're disabled. The very people who would hold a door open for you are the ones you would never expect. The kid who looks like he's nothing but trouble will do it, but the woman who is exceedingly well dressed and should know better will slam the door on you. It leaves you in a topsy-turvy place, realizing that you can't come to judgment too quickly.

Rehab

For my legs to function perfectly — to bend and unbend — it took nine years. My doctor made me do many things considered unusual in those days. I never had a steroidal drug. I never had cortisone. He said, "You have youth. You have time on your side. We're going to do this differently." He starved me for thirty-one days, allowing me to consume only grapes and distilled water. Then, slowly, we'd bring back certain food groups. I probably didn't eat beef or drink coffee for about twenty-five years. It was very unusual, but it worked.

I also had this really tough physiotherapist. I always imagined she would have played a major role in the Gestapo. I thought, "Oh my heavens, this is a torturous individual!" She treated me with ice, which was very painful because it felt as though my legs were burning. I felt she was not a person with much heart. But the day I unbent my legs for the first time, she wept.

The Postgraduate

While this was happening to my body, I still had to keep up with my studies. It was very difficult because we were living in a basement flat and the cost of transportation to and from the university wasn't covered.

After my master's in the education of exceptional children it came time to decide on a doctoral program. In what field could I be independent, make a life for myself, and call the shots? There were certain obvious hurdles that had an influence on where I could go: I certainly didn't have the luxury of going anywhere beyond Saskatoon. I decided on clinical psychology.

Once I enrolled, even though I was fully accepted into the doctoral program, the department decided to change the rules retroactively, not wanting to allow someone into the program without a master's in the field. I was required to do another master's degree, this time in psychology, at the same time as doing my doctoral program.

I became the first student to finish my dissertation before going away on the required internship program, which I did at the Clarke Institute in Toronto. When I came back, I had completed all the doctoral coursework, my comprehensive exams, the master's program, the equivalent of my thesis, and

I had defended my dissertation. At the end of it all, after receiving my PhD, I looked back and realized I had created a life for myself. "I am a citizen here," I realized. "I'm not some kid who just arrived on the scene and decided to start making the world a better place." I didn't believe in social-working the world.

I felt that I would be a much better university teacher, as well as a therapist and a researcher, if I kept my life more complete. I was very busy, joining several boards of directors. The professors at the department saw these involvements as distractions. The only reason they kept me on was that I received an unprecedented number of Canada Council research fellowships, getting one every year I was there.

Lessons

I learned early on that success is not about anything grand; it simply means getting up every time you fall. You have to make what's in front of you count for something. And if it only makes life tougher — so what?

Everybody thinks that we're supposed to say to someone who's graduating, "I wish you nothing but happiness." Well, I don't! What I wish for them is a full life. A truly rich life. You're going to have joy and you're going to have pain, you'll have moments that are indescribable — all the beauty of what life can bring — and you'll have moments of grief: that's what living a full life means. I wouldn't want to keep people from the hurtful lessons because I believe they enrich your life and make it what it is.

EDDIE GREENSPAN

"All these young lawyers want to go smell the roses.
Fine — smell the roses, but not at the risk of doing a mediocre job."

What do Conrad Black, Garth Drabinsky, a Quebec Hells Angel, and Robert Latimer have in common? All have been defended in court by **Eddie Greenspan**. Renowned for his bravado and common touch as much as for his motley client list, Greenspan is Canada's best-known defence lawyer.

Growing up in Niagara Falls, Ontario, Greenspan was attracted to what he calls the "show business" of criminal law. He loved the grand cross-examinations and jury addresses he read about in books and saw on *Perry Mason*. Shortly after coming to national prominence as the junior counsel in wealthy developer Peter Demeter's 1974 murder trial, Greenspan co-founded his own law firm, Greenspan, Gold and Moldaver. Thereafter, he amassed a hefty list of high-profile clients, fought the Mulroney government's plan to re-impose the death penalty, and gained further exposure on the CBC Radio series *The Scales of Justice*.

Early Years

My father had gone to law school during the Second World War, but, after meeting my mother, he dropped out and went home to take over the family scrapyard; he never went back to school. A month after my thirteenth birthday, he had a massive heart attack and died. The night he was taken away, I sat in our family den, upset and confused, looking at his library. I took one of the books off the shelf and began to read. It was the life story of Clarence Darrow, one of the greatest criminal lawyers that ever practised. By the time I finished the book, I knew I had an opportunity to live out my father's unfulfilled dream.

From that day on, there was nothing for me but the pursuit of the law. I thought of nothing else and became absorbed by notions of justice, fairness, and the relationship between the state and the individual — questioning when the state should interfere with an individual's life. The idea that a criminal lawyer stands between intrusiveness and individual liberty was especially fascinating.

I also learned from my environment. Niagara Falls was a tough town. A number of people with whom I went to school had serious difficulties with the law and a few ended up in jail. It intrigued me that, given our similar backgrounds, some of us were on one side of the law and some were on the other. Why was that? I knew the people that got into trouble and realized they weren't nearly as bad as the system was making them out to be.

Coming to Toronto

I wanted to get out of Niagara Falls, to go around the horseshoe and be exposed to life in the big city. When I enrolled at the University of Toronto for my undergraduate degree, it was like a whole new world: at home we received the *Globe and Mail* a day after its publication; here, I was getting it at ten o'clock the night before. All of a sudden, there was a sense of immediacy in the news. Compared to Niagara Falls, this was like New York City.

By then, the family scrapyard was bankrupt and my mother had gone back to being a secretary at a public school, which generated the family's sole income. When I came back for the summer, I was able to find a job emptying parking meters for the municipality of Niagara Falls. At night, I'd go back to City Hall and count all the nickels, pennies, and dimes. The position opened up to university students because the full-time guy had been caught stealing and went to jail. I've always been thankful for crime. You could say it gave me my first summer job.

Osgoode Hall Law School

The first year of law school was the most important. I was exposed to the rhythm of the law, learning how to read cases and being subjected to a new form of learning, a different kind of literature. Though I was often bored, it taught me how to read the law, which takes time because I needed to process the words of a case and see where it fit into the grand scheme of things.

The second year was spent honing those skills. The stakes got higher. You realized that once you're out of law school, you're on your own, so you have to develop good patterns of habit. It also exposes you to different areas of the law.

My third year was a complete and utter waste of time. I learned nothing new. All the students were just going through the motions. In my opinion, it should be cut altogether.

Criminal law continued to be my passion. During my studies, I worked every year in a law firm, where I probably spent more time than I did in school. I was so focused that, though I never missed a single criminal law class, it would be closer to the truth to say I hardly attended anything else.

Because I had a goal since the age of thirteen, I never learned the difference between dream and reality. None of the lawyers who wrote books about their great jury addresses ever mentioned that it required fifty lonely, tough, hard-working hours to prepare a magnificent one-hour peroration. No one taught us how to do that. Had I known that at thirteen, I might have stayed in the family scrap business.

Law School Today

Tuition increases have made law school much less accessible. Also — having been a law professor at Osgoode Hall and the University of Toronto for almost thirty years — I have seen students change. Now, they all look for "quality of life," trying to succeed in law and achieve a balanced lifestyle. As an avowed workaholic, I know that if they want to be good lawyers, they'll have to work incredibly hard. Nothing comes easy.

All these young lawyers want to go smell the roses. Fine — smell the roses, but not at the risk of doing a mediocre job. Though it may not be obvious at first, there are untold hours one has to put in. I may prepare fifty hours to do a fifteen-minute cross-examination. It might not be worth the fifty hours — maybe I could have done it in twelve — but I don't know that until after the cross-examination.

At the end of the day, my general philosophy was never to care about what was going on around me; I simply did what I needed to do. These days, law schools foster a herd mentality. Individuality has become less apparent than it was forty years ago.

Coming out of academia, I got any economist's dream job: working at the U.S. Federal Reserve Board. It was an incredibly exciting time to be there, because the entire banking system was changing. Inflation was brewing and no one knew what to do about it. When the new chairman, Paul Volcker, limited the money supply and interest rates began to soar, the home builders industry and the farmers were burning him in effigy in the streets. One lunatic actually snuck into the boardroom with a machete, intent on killing him.

I was right in the thick of the chaos. Because I had been hired to work on capital markets, a field that was hugely important at the time, I managed to become a briefer at the Monday morning meetings. Those were the most intense pressure cookers I have ever experienced. The Fed worked me to death seven days a week, but I loved it. Young people today often aren't prepared to do whatever it takes to shine. They set their own career boundaries. In the end, that's probably a good thing. I think my generation saw the pendulum swing too widely on the workaholic side.

— **Sherry Cooper**, chief economist at BMO Capital Markets and author of *Ride the Wave: Taking Control in the Acceleration Age*

The First Case

School had made me an expert in criminal law. But what did I know about "lawyering"? Nothing. During my first trial, for example, I wanted to object to a question being asked but had no idea how to do it. I stood up and waited for the judge to acknowledge me in front of the jury. He didn't even look over. The question was asked and answered and I was standing there looking like a jerk. I reached over and poured a glass of water to make it seem like that was why I stood up. I learned pretty quickly that if you want to object, you stand up and say, "I object!"

That's why lawyering is something for which law school cannot prepare you. Though it's possible to *teach* advocacy, it can't be *learned*. You either have an instinct for it or you don't. When you're cross-examining somebody, you need to know not to ask certain questions. And what it comes down to is a combination of experience, nature, and intuition.

For that case, I was representing the appeal of a young man who had been convicted for possessing tools supposedly used for housebreaking. The judge wouldn't stop yelling at me. I kept being told to sit down, even when I hadn't made all my points. He called me "Green*spoon*," "Green*burg*," and "Green*stein*." At one point I got really annoyed. "My lord," I said, "my name is Green*span*!" He looked at me and said, "I don't care *what* your name is. Sit down!"

I won the appeal and my client was given a retrial. That was a tremendous experience in terms of understanding people and recognizing what I could and could not do. In my jury address at the retrial, for example, I used the word "surreptitiously." I looked at those twelve people and knew that not one of them understood me. I vowed to never again use a word not commonly appreciated by everyone. The use of the word "purport" should be a criminal offence. It's language I don't want to know. To use legal expressions and lawyer-talk is like pretending to be something I'm not. Lawyers like to project an air of respectability because of a desire for respect. But I believe you earn respect by being yourself. My first trial taught me that I couldn't be anybody else; I could only be me.

I came to respect every single client of mine. As a lawyer, I may have many cases, but each of my clients has only one, the most important case of their lives. If he's a truck driver charged with impaired driving, it's his job on the line. If it's a serious murder, he may be going to jail for a long time. That first case wasn't too important in the grand scheme of things, but for me it was the biggest eye-opener of my life. I treated it like a capital murder trial and have done the same for every other case since.

Learning on the Job

Many times, when someone's charged with a crime, there isn't a police officer involved who doesn't think the accused is guilty; there isn't a prosecutor who doesn't think he's guilty; there isn't a judge who doesn't think he's guilty. Often, there isn't a jury member who doesn't think he's guilty either. Generally, the only ones prepared to give him the benefit of the doubt are the accused's mother and me, the lawyer. Sometimes, my *own* mother believes the person I'm representing is guilty.

As hopeless as it seems, persistence is vital. In law, no presupposition or prejudice is beyond attack. Every rule can change. There are no immutable truths. Before somebody developed the "battered woman syndrome" as a defence for murdering one's husband while he's asleep, the science of law would have required a serious threat of bodily harm. But law is more than a science; it is also an art. Basic rules can be altered. I've fought against rules that have existed for 150 years and changed them. The boundaries are constantly being moved, based on fairness and justice. The law is not — nor can it ever be — a simple question of black and white.

On Money

When I got married, my wife and I were in serious debt. She had four years of student loans and I had seven: we owed a ton of money. When I only made $12,000 my first year, we began to have serious doubts about getting out of it. How could I possibly stay in Toronto? I was seriously considering going back to Niagara Falls, practising real estate and corporate commercial law, and giving up my dream, but my wife was committed. "Let's stay one more year," she said. "Try it out and see how it goes. If, at the end, it still doesn't work out, then you can go back." It was only about halfway through that second year that my practice started to blossom. Success came very suddenly. I still didn't get out of debt, though, in terms of carrying the baggage of my student loans, until I was thirty-one — six years later.

I genuinely hate debt. When I bought a house, I did everything I could to avoid having a mortgage, not wanting to owe any money at all. Being debt-free added greatly to my freedom. It's a very old-fashioned sensibility, rooted in my upbringing, that I've tried to maintain throughout my life. Even though I've acquired more things, I've always tried to avoid being in debt.

I also made a deal with my family. "Let me do what I want," I said, "because

Eddie Greenspan and his wife, Suzy: "I was seriously considering going back to Niagara Falls, practising real estate and corporate commercial law, and giving up my dream, but my wife was committed."

the law is my first love. I'm married to it. You're a casual mistress. This is my life. The quid pro quo is that you get all the financial benefits." I stayed true to my word: the building I work in, for example, does not belong to me; it belongs to my wife.

Winning and losing meant everything to me. Money meant very little. I've often said that if my wife didn't have an interest in money, we'd still be living in a rental apartment. I've been to all the three-star Michelin restaurants, but I'll always prefer a hamburger. That's just my personality.

KAREN KAIN

"Whenever I was singled out for my abilities or a teacher would focus on me too much, there would be resentment. I could really feel it."

It starts early. At four years of age, girls begin taking lessons. If they are good — if they have the endurance, the delicacy, and the right body type — they are placed in specialized schools. From that day on, the work is intensive, consisting almost entirely of study, rehearsal, and performance. When they graduate, they will have spent little time doing anything else. Their career goals are set: they will become ballerinas. For **Karen Kain**, this was the way it went. Born in Hamilton, Ontario, she spent her childhood dancing and her adolescence training at Canada's National Ballet School. After graduating at eighteen, she was selected for the prestigious company of the National Ballet and began her career as a professional ballerina.

Kain went on to become Canada's best-known — and most internationally successful — dancer. She was a silver medallist in the Moscow International Ballet Competition, is a recipient of the Order of Canada, and holds honorary degrees from five Canadian universities. She retired from dancing in 1997 and in 2005 returned to the National Ballet as its artistic director.

Starting Out at the National Ballet

My early success was unusual. I was chosen out of the *corps de ballet* to dance a leading role when I was very young. The artistic director of the National Ballet, Celia Franca, decided that she was going to put me in *Swan Lake* because the lead ballerina was injured. The leading roles require such stamina and strength that they usually go to established performers. Being nineteen and getting to do a classic like *Swan Lake* doesn't happen very often.

As a result, there was some bitterness from the other dancers. Throughout my career, whenever I was singled out for my abilities or a teacher would focus on me too much, there would be resentment. I could really feel it. Sometimes it affected me badly because I wanted people to like me.

A Certain Obsession

During my twenties, I started to become more aware of things outside the ballet world. There were increasing demands made of us to be better actors, more "interesting" on stage, and generally well-rounded human beings. We had to develop an awareness of other people's lives, as well as our own, and bring that understanding to our work. It made us better artists.

Until then, ballet had been the way you identified yourself: it was who you were, the reason you got out of bed in the morning, and the reason you trained all day. The truth is, ballet demands a certain obsession. You can't succeed unless you're obsessive. Even as you become aware of external things, it never changes your commitment to the art form.

If it goes too far, it can become dangerous. It's important for young artists to have balanced lives. Even though that seems like a cliché, it's true. You need to connect with the outside, especially by making non-dance friends. Your career is so short that by the time you hit thirty, you're already pushing the limits. When I became professional after high school, I knew that I only had a short time to have a career. As a result, I never had a home life and I didn't have a relationship outside the company. There was no time, no space, and I wasn't the least bit interested.

We were doing eight shows a week, on tour five months a year, and in New York one month every summer. We rehearsed all day, danced all night, and slept on buses. I loved it, never feeling like I needed anything else. Only at the end of my twenties did I start to realize there might be more to life. It dawned on me that maybe this wasn't everything. So I started to make friends outside the company, go on vacations, and be more like a "normal" person. Being a ballerina is a very self-centred kind of life, and at a certain point, that becomes unsatisfying.

Performance

I was always a nervous performer, a fact that didn't change throughout my career. Controlling my fear was an important skill, since the most satisfying thing about being a performer was to finally be in front of thousands of people without embarrassing myself. With a large audience, things became heightened. If you've ever tried to speak to a crowd, you know how self-conscious you can be, wondering if you'll trip and other things you wouldn't even think of if no one was watching.

As a kid, every time the doorbell would ring, I'd run up to my room and hide. Even in my twenties, I was painfully shy. I never opened my mouth. That's just the way I was. It became worse as a professional. The more acclaim I'd get for my work, the more afraid I got. The pressure was unbearable. I went through periods where I lost confidence and didn't want to go on stage because I didn't think I could meet expectations. People had heard so much about me, bought tickets, and were expecting something. I was quite

Karen Kain: "Ballet demands a certain obsession."

convinced that I couldn't give them what they wanted. It felt like there was some kind of mistake — and I was going to get found out.

I used to imagine this place where I would be watching myself from a distance and judging myself, saying, "Hey, that wasn't nearly as good as in rehearsal." It's hard for your mind to blot out all the distractions with so much adrenaline rushing through you. You need to feel it happening and still focus your mind. The skill is to be able to enter a cast-iron place where all the things that can take away your concentration don't penetrate. It took me years to get there, to know I could put that voice out of my mind.

The part I enjoyed most was using my imagination. It was likely because of my shyness: instead of being me, I wanted to be all the characters I got to play. The way they moved was also part of creating. Whether as women or birds, it didn't matter. They weren't me. They were facets of me. It's like being an actress, only instead of words to express myself, I used my physicality.

Nureyev

It was early in my career when Rudolf Nureyev came along. I was probably twenty-one. He came to dance with the National Ballet of Canada, and his first day in the studio, he pointed at me. "That one!" he said. "I want that one to be the leading role." But Celia Franca thought I was too inexperienced and didn't cast me with him in *Sleeping Beauty*.

Nureyev kept pushing her and rehearsing me on tour until finally I made my debut in Houston. This was against the will of Celia, who felt I was too young. But he just wouldn't hear of it. He took me under his wing and, on my holidays, would take me to dance around the world with him. He became my mentor and my inspiration.

Though extremely demanding, he was good to me. He'd bully me in an affectionate way, pushing me to do things I didn't think I could do. That was one of the greatest aspects of working with him. He showed me how much further I could go with my own abilities. Because he pushed himself too, he was the only one who was as much of a perfectionist as I was. I guess he recognized a soulmate on that level. As long as I measured up — as long as I gave him what he was expecting in terms of performance, energy, and commitment — he didn't complain. Nureyev was someone I loved pleasing, and because his admiration was such a big deal, it was a motivating force for me.

He stayed with the company for a decade and we worked with him every year, sometimes for six months, sometimes for only a month. In the beginning, we did long tours together, and as I matured, I started dancing in more of his productions. He would simply invite me to come and be his partner and we would dance together in the main opera houses of Europe and the rest of the world.

Problems

Then I became dependent. When Nureyev wasn't around, I would lose my confidence and wouldn't dance my best. Suddenly, I couldn't do half the stuff I did when he was there. It was a really rough time in my career and I had to grow up a lot. My performances got worse, and people started calling me on it. When that started, I lost even more confidence. It was hard having a career in the spotlight. One day, they were pronouncing wonderful things about me in the press, which freaked me out because I never thought I measured up. Then, a few years later, when they called me a has-been who hadn't fulfilled their expectations, I started to believe them.

At that point I had to learn to stop seeking people's approval. I stopped trying to please Nureyev, the press, and the public. "If I'm going to keep dancing," I thought, "I have to do it because I want to, not because I'm concerned about

I'm struck by how well balanced medical students have become. They all come to medicine with very different backgrounds. Many of them have undergraduate degrees behind them. The problem is that, though older and more mature, they're too aware of the outside world to be able to put the blinders on and work persistently on a single narrow objective. In my day, we didn't have that. We took what was given to us.

— **Philippe Couillard**, Minister of Health and Social Services, Quebec what others think." It sounds simple, but it was a vital lesson for me.

I stopped dancing for almost a year to sort myself out. I even went to a psychiatrist. In the end, I decided I really did want to dance — and I wasn't going to do it for anybody else. I needed to go through a lot to get to that point, and to feel like I wanted to brave it again. When I came back to ballet, though a little rocky at first, I never had the same problem. In order to reach that level — and to keep dancing for the rest of my career — I needed to have some kind of crisis.

BRIAN MULRONEY

"In politics, setbacks can be very helpful."

Brian Mulroney, Canada's eighteenth prime minister, grew up along the St. Lawrence in the small town of Baie-Comeau, Quebec. The community was centred around a mill owned by the Quebec North Shore Paper Company, which employed a large segment of its three thousand residents. Though raised by Irish Catholic parents, Mulroney had no difficulty conversing in the language of the town's francophone majority. His attachment to Baie-Comeau ran deep: as a teenager, he had seriously considered joining the mill's apprenticeship program — a path that would have taught him to become a carpenter or, like his father, an electrician. He was discouraged by his father. "The only way out of a paper mill town," he was told, "is through a university door."

Heeding the advice, Mulroney went to St. Francis Xavier University in Nova Scotia for his bachelor's degree, followed by a four-year law program at the Université Laval in Quebec City. After a decade of private practice, he ran for the leadership of the Progressive Conservative Party in 1976, only to be defeated by Joe Clark. Then, in 1983, Mulroney ran again and won. The next year, he led the party to the largest majority government in Canadian history, winning 211 of 282 seats in the House of Commons. During his nine years as prime minister, he was integral in bringing Canada into the North American Free Trade Agreement, combatting the environmental problem of acid rain, and attempting to overhaul the constitutional status quo at Meech Lake.

Early Politics

I guess I'd always been a good student. But by the time I got to St. Francis Xavier, I became increasingly attracted to politics and, inappropriately, spent far too little time in the library. When I began university in 1955, all the political parties were recruiting new students across campus. What was especially interesting about the Progressive Conservatives was that they were the underdogs. Both provincially and federally, the Liberals had been in power for about twenty years. I was attracted to Bob Stanfield, leader of the opposition in Nova Scotia, at one level, and on the other, John Diefenbaker, who was about to lead the party in Ottawa. I also found their ideas fit well with my view of the world.

As a youth delegate, I attended the 1956 Progressive Conservative convention. The party was choosing its next leader and I put my support behind Diefenbaker. He was a very electrifying figure. He was a great speaker and had a well-articulated vision for Canada's North. He took me — and the country — by storm.

Eventually becoming executive vice-president of the party's student federation, I was able to stay in touch with Diefenbaker. While he was leader of the opposition, then prime minister, I would go to Ottawa at his invitation and see him in his parliamentary office from time to time. Even in private, he was quite inspirational and exciting.

It was not that unusual for an important politician to meet with lowly students. In my case, it was because I was active in politics and consistently supported him. I was vice-chairman of Youth for Diefenbaker for Atlantic Canada. I wouldn't say he knew me intimately, but we were able to have some interesting political discussions. He even spurred me to make recommendations. His example — as a curious and open leader who met with young supporters — was one I tried to follow when I was in office.

Learning Canada

Later, as a result of the friendships I'd established in the party, I was able to get a job as private secretary for Alvin Hamilton, the federal minister of agriculture. He had just recovered from an attack of Bell's palsy and needed someone to help him in his office while he focused on an upcoming election campaign. I wound up on the Prairies and ventured to places as far-flung as the Peace River Valley and Fort St. John, British Columbia.

Until then, I knew very little about Canada. Baie-Comeau was a largely French-speaking town with a smaller English-speaking community. Everyone mixed, intermarried, and was fully bilingual. I had thought it was like that across the country. I figured if we were doing it in Baie-Comeau, then everyone else was too. When I worked for Alvin Hamilton, I realized how vastly different

Alberta and British Columbia were from Eastern Canada. Only then did I acquire an understanding of the diversity and breadth of the country.

Law School

Even with my political distractions, I was still able to get through St. Francis Xavier with honours. I won an entrance scholarship to the law faculty at Dalhousie University. I attended for a year — and enjoyed it greatly — but decided to transfer to a law school in Quebec. Had I graduated in Nova Scotia, I wouldn't have been able to practise law in my home province. I had a deep attachment to Quebec — the place where I was born and raised. Having been away for so long, my French was getting quite rusty. Besides, Dalhousie only taught us common law and I wanted to learn Quebec civil law. So, I transferred to the Université Laval in Quebec City.

I've never regretted my decision. It was quite an exciting time to be a student in that city. The Quiet Revolution, the change that catapulted Quebec from a traditional Catholic society to a modern nationalist one, had just begun. The Laval students spent a lot of time at the Assemblée Nationale debates and the courthouses to hear the Royal Commissions that were underway. We were very much caught up in the excitement of the period. We all lived in the *vieux quartier* and rubbed shoulders with politicians and other noteworthy personalities. Again — though I wasn't the only one — I spent too much time on extracurricular activities and not enough on my studies. I regret it now, but it was hard to do differently in those days.

The crop of interesting people that came out of my first-year law class was probably unprecedented in Canadian political history: from a future minister — André Ouellette — and a future premier — Lucien Bouchard — to a future chief of staff — Bernard Roy — and a future senator — Michael Meighen — as well as many judges. One classmate, Peter White, even organized a national conference entitled the Congress on Canadian Affairs, in which the rest of us were all involved. Most of the work I did as prime minister trying to alter Canada's Constitution originated in the ideas of that conference. Those four years at Laval were definitely — and I think most of my former classmates would agree — the most exciting and interesting of our lives.

Decisions

Upon graduation, I was recruited to join the law firm of Ogilvy Renault in Montreal. It was the largest firm in Canada at the time. They had apparently heard of me at Laval, since I was fairly prominent as a politically minded student. They called me and said, "We're looking for people who are fully bilingual and who've had good training." I had no intention of going. My plan was to practise law back home. "I'm going back to Baie-Comeau," I told them. "Well," they said, "why don't you come and speak with us." I went to their offices in Montreal, met their senior partners, and was offered a job. So I consulted with my father. "You can always come home," he said, "but this is a unique opportunity. Why don't you give it a try?"

I moved up to Montreal but wasn't sure whether I'd stay. It was my first time living there and I didn't know anybody. I had also never been associated with a huge organization before. It was altogether a brand new experience.

All I did was what I had done in the past. At Laval, I had learned to focus on my responsibilities, work hard, and meet due dates. I applied those lessons to Ogilvy Renault and things began well.

Unfortunately, within the first year, my father passed away. I had to help my mother and my younger siblings. I moved them all into my apartment in Montreal and we had to start over again with very little money until we were able to put my siblings through college. That became another incentive to put my head down and work hard. Any political aspirations I may have had in those first ten years had to be put on hold until much later.

Running for the Party Leadership

I guess you could say I had a natural ability to make friends. I enjoyed meeting people and, as a bachelor during my twenties, had time to socialize. I was able to float around. I developed an association of friends, many of whom are still close to me today. I was a natural "networker" (a term that didn't exist back then), but I also worked at it. I didn't take anything for granted, including someone's friendship: I always tried to reciprocate. Sometimes, through

Anyone who wants to join the Foreign Service needs to have a sense of adventure, a sense of history, and a sense of imagination. While being flexible, you also need a certain integrity — to know what you stand for. Flexibility doesn't mean being wishy-washy. If you're comfortable in your skin, you'll be a good Foreign Service officer.

One of my early postings as a diplomat was in Beirut. While I was there, a gang of terrorists took over the embassy and held us captive. I had an AK-47 pointed at my stomach for nine hours. During that experience, my guiding principle was that nobody should die — including the hijackers. I tried to avoid being too rigid. I never wanted to say, "We'll never give in to terrorism," even if that meant people would die. It wouldn't have worked. Instead, by making some promises we knew the government couldn't keep, we were able to get out alive. I guess I was confident enough to know that was our best hope.

— **Alan Sullivan**, former Canadian ambassador to Italy, Austria, and Ireland and former consul general to New York no planning of my own, social friendships turned into political ones.

An example of that came later, in 1976, when I ran for the leadership of the Progressive Conservatives. I had some friends who'd encouraged me in the pursuit. They said they'd form a finance committee and raise some money for me. The next thing I knew, I was running for national office. And when that happens, you have to be prepared to accept the outcome. In my case, I lost.

It was a hard lesson. I started from nowhere, as the only serious candidate yet to be elected to the House of Commons. I was way behind the pack and wound up second on the first ballot. Having come that close, it was even more difficult when I lost on the final ballot. Had I come in sixth, I would have considered it a pleasant experience. But because I came so close, the letdown was hard to take.

Still, had I not run and lost, I would have never won in 1983. In politics, setbacks can be very helpful. The key is to learn from your mistakes, focus on your interests, and be aware of your abilities. Without the experience of defeat, your interests tend to be very unfocused. Once life has dealt you a significant event, you develop the focus and discipline needed to move your agenda forward.

ANNETTE VERSCHUREN

"The thing that kept me stable was a continuing self-respect."

After her father had a serious heart attack, a thirteen-year-old **Annette Verschuren** was forced, along with her siblings, to take over the affairs of the family farm on Cape Breton Island. Her adolescence included regular high school pastimes — classes, parties, and sports — as well as agricultural chores, from birthing calves to arranging the farm's finances. After finishing university, the transition to the business world came naturally, requiring both persistence and the ability to balance multiple activities.

Though it wasn't always easy, Verschuren moved steadily up the corporate ladder and, in 1996, became the president of Home Depot Canada. Though working in an office building from which she claims can be had "the best views in all Toronto," she is still attached to the two most important things in her life: family and home. Every year, she pays for a two-week vacation in Mexico for all her relatives and still makes countless regular trips back to Cape Breton.

Challenged in a Negative Way

I never knew what I wanted to do with my life. In Grade 12, I took a career guidance assessment and it came back saying that, based on my strengths, I should be an accountant. I didn't even know what an accountant was. Luckily, my guidance counsellor gave different advice. "Your older sister's a teacher," she said. "Maybe that's what you should be."

Following her suggestion, I decided to go into arts at St. Francis Xavier University in Antigonish. I soon got bored. The next year, I switched — without telling my parents — into business. It was a much better fit. A business degree was more valuable, and the experience helped me in two important areas: to find focus and to develop discipline. Those really guided my career. Without them, I would have had a limited future.

My social skills were highly developed. It was critical, from high school on, to have good interpersonal skills. In Grade 9, I was head of student council, and even though I'd never sewed in my life, I won the end-of-year award for the school's best "home economist," which sounds like a joke, but I still have the trophy to prove it. The award I'm most proud of came from my university days: for downing a pint of beer in four seconds. To compensate for my love of partying, though, I had to rely on being a good crammer when it came to studying.

The reason for my development had a lot to do with growing up on a farm between two brothers, never knowing I was different. I didn't hit discrimination — or perceived discrimination — until I took a business course in which I did poorly. I went to see the teacher, who hadn't impressed me much, and asked what I could do to improve my marks. He said I should probably go into "secretarial arts." Apparently, women weren't made for business.

I looked at the guy and said, "I couldn't disagree with you more." That sort of thing fortified me to go further and I ended up doing well in the class. I loved being challenged in a negative way because I could turn it into a positive and use it to move forward.

Illness

Until I was twenty-eight, I had severe health problems. I was in the hospital for at least a couple of weeks every year. As a teenager, I had been diagnosed with a hereditary kidney condition and had four operations between the ages of fifteen and twenty-one. It was after the third operation that I woke up and realized that having a healthy life was pretty darn important. It gave me great perspective. In order to regulate the problem, I had to work hard at it and take good care of myself. If I was abusive to my body, I would never be healthy again. So I had to stop playing sports and — more importantly — quit my wild lifestyle.

As a teenager, I loved to party. Then, a Montreal nun named Rolande Ouimet changed my life. When I was twenty, she listened to me sing and believed I had enough talent to become a good musician. She allowed me to become one of her pupils. Even though she was a nun — and, having gone to Catholic school my whole life, I hated nuns — she was a well-educated and open-minded human being. She taught me self-discipline and self-belief.

Everything turned around after I met her. She told me not to smoke or drink, to go to bed early, and to take care of my health. Every Monday morning, she asked me what I had done over the weekend. If I'd been partying, she would drill me for it. She forced me to sing three hours a day and take piano classes for another four. It was hard work, but I didn't mind. Someone had finally channelled my talent.

— **Rosemarie Landry**, former opera singer and music professor at the Université de Montréal

These days, if I feel bad about something, I always relate it to the moment I woke up in the recovery room. I jump out of bed every morning figuring I've been given another day to live.

The Cape Breton Development Corporation

Four companies wanted to hire me out of university, including an accounting firm and a radio station, but I wanted to work for a particular coal mining company back home. Four people from my graduating class applied for the job at the Cape Breton Development Corporation, some with connections in the mining business. I thought my chances of getting it were pretty slim. I did my homework and spent three days preparing for the interview. I read all the annual reports of the corporation and became very informed. When I went in for the interview, I spent an hour and a half telling the guy what I'd do to turn the Cape Breton tourism industry around. That just blew him away. They gave me the job. It taught me the four critical factors to succeed in an interview: be prepared, be knowledgeable, respect your interviewer, and be clear about the direction you want the organization to take.

I was twenty-one when I started working there and had an amazing time. I was involved in trying to leverage the coal mining industry by supporting secondary businesses in Cape Breton. Because the company was central to the area, they needed to set up secondary industries and create jobs for displaced workers in order to make the region more diverse for the working population. There were many industries I tried to develop for this purpose — including metal fabrication plants, sawmills, and tourism — helping them expand, working with them on business plans, and securing government loans. The work seemed to enrich the area. I remember giving a loan to a woman who wanted to buy a sewing machine and start a business — a business that is still operating today.

When I started, I was in way over my head and didn't have a clue. But I loved drowning in situations: those were the environments in which I thrived. Often my boss would invite me into his office. "Look," he'd say. "I don't know how to do this. You figure it out and develop a program on your own." That's what I would do; and for three years I was the only woman working in an extraordinarily male-dominated business.

Then I was transferred to the coal side, the corporation's primary industry, as director of planning, and, eventually, assistant to the president. They would continually put me in pressure situations. Since we were a Crown corporation, we had to deal with top levels of the federal government in Ottawa. I remember one particular presentation when my boss didn't have the confidence to get up in front of a group of deputy ministers and convince them to spend more money in our sector. I had to do it instead. Here I was, twenty-seven years old, answering all sorts of questions on the viability of an underground coal mining operation in Cape Breton. It was fascinating. Of the four presidents I had in two years, I survived them all.

The Next Step

When I left the corporation, I was twenty-nine and still living at home. Having seen how badly public companies were run, I joined the Canada Development Investment Corporation, an arm of the federal government that worked on privatizing Crown corporations. I became executive vice-president of the organization, working with the greatest businesspeople, accountants, and lawyers in Canada. We helped the privatization of fishery products, Canadair, and de Havilland, working very closely with the federal bureaucrats. It was going to be a six-month contract, and it turned into six years.

Then I joined Imasco as vice-president for corporate development. I made a deal with them. "I'll do this job," I said, "but I want operational experience. You have retail operations, so let me run something." Often women get pigeonholed in administrative positions where they can't go anywhere; I didn't want my career to hit a dead end. My confidence was high. I knew I could physically manage assets — from my experience running the family farm — so why couldn't I manage a retail enterprise?

They honoured their commitment and I soon became involved in the retail industry. I didn't squander the opportunity, putting together a proposal for a deal with the United States, selling off eleven stores, and turning the company around. Then I left to work for Michaels, a crafts retailer, founding sixteen stores in Canada in twenty-six months. When Home Depot approached, making me two serious offers before I finally accepted, I was ready to try something new.

While jumping from job to job in a career that has been all over the map — both geographically and professionally — the thing that kept me stable was a continuing self-respect. I have always valued my own soul. I was married with a good relationship, spent a great deal of time with my family, and have always gotten along with my friends, but I've never been owned by anybody or anything, which I think is critically important.

"A lot of people have to learn that lesson: that somebody in a position of experience and authority may be completely wrong."

Until she spoke with her high school guidance counsellor, **Valerie Pringle** had no idea what she wanted to do with her life. A news junky with a penchant for current affairs, Pringle had never considered a career in media. Thanks to her counsellor's encouragement, however, she applied to the radio and television arts program at Toronto's Ryerson Polytechnical Institute (now Ryerson University). After falling in love with radio, Pringle fought relentlessly to get her foot in the door at a local station.

In 1984 she made the transition to television, as co-host of CBC's *Midday*. In 1991, she moved to the successful CTV morning show *Canada AM*. Her career continues in full throttle: she is host of *Canadian Antiques Roadshow* and *Valerie Pringle Has Left the Building*. In 2007, she was a recipient of the Order of Canada.

Good Qualities

I never expected to end up in radio. I studied it in my first year of journalism at Ryerson. Then I did television and film. I remember being the biggest frigging disaster in film and carrying around a tripod and light stand while the other students made a short movie. It was my only project. "I hate it!" I said. "I'm not good at it!" It's so useful to know what you hate. Figuring out what you like can be hard, so anything that can help narrow it down is great. I went right back to the department and asked if I could do another session in radio.

At the end of that year, I found out about a summer job with one of Toronto's major radio stations, CFRB. They had a program called "Good News Reporters" and they were going to hire eight kids for the summer. Even though I'd only taken a few radio courses, I was damned if I wasn't going to be one of them. I was very aggressive about going after that job. They asked for a sample of what I could do as a reporter, so I put together a little story about the McMichael collection in Kleinburg, Ontario — how cool it was that you could go and peer through a window into Tom Thomson's old cabin. One of the students at Ryerson helped me with it because I was never the greatest technical genius.

I also happened to live near the CFRB offices. On my walk to school, I'd pass underneath the news director's window and wave at him. Ultimately, I met him at a function. "Oh, I'm sorry," he told me. "I haven't listened to your tape yet. Give me a call in a week or two."

So I did. My parents never pressured me to call. It was just in my personality. I wanted the job, so I called. I find that different from my own kids who are far more reticent. "What do I do?" "What do I say?" "Maybe you could tell me what to say." And I'll tell them, "Without being a stalker, be keen, be enthusiastic, and be aggressive." Those are good qualities. People recognize that and sometimes they need a reminder. That's how I got my first job.

Good News Reporters

At CFRB, they wanted us to do happy, positive stories. It was their way of bridging the generation gap, letting young people do pieces at the end of each news broadcast. The listeners were supposed to say, "Oh, isn't that sweet" or "That's cute." It was a nice addition to what they had, which was generally done by an older crowd.

In that bygone Trudeau age, they were handing out money to any group of kids who wanted to put a summer carnival on in their backyard. It was called an Opportunity for Youth grant. Everybody got one! Money was falling off the trees. Well, it was a great source of stories for us. We would interview some poor soul — actually some rich soul — who just got a government grant to pursue his or her project. Classic stuff for youth stories.

With my little Sony microphone I was able to interview some pretty interesting young people, whether it was Steve Podborski after he won his first downhill ski race at fourteen, the guys who opened the first Roots store in Toronto, Garth Drabinsky when he started practising entertainment law, or Rob Prichard when he was dean of the University of Toronto Law School in his twenties.

It was a wonderful summer employment program. While I was back at Ryerson, finishing my third and final year, CFRB hired me to do little jobs: to report from the Royal Winter Fair and things like that. It worked well for me — and for them, because I was a young voice finding interesting stories. Towards the end of the year, they said, "Look, when you graduate, we're going to create a job for you."

It was magnificent. When I graduated, I became a full-time youth reporter, doing stories similar to what the Good News Reporters did, and Coca-Cola sponsored the whole thing. During that time, I realized how much I loved radio. It's immediate, informal, intimate, and a wonderful form of communication. Prior to that, I would have still preferred television.

The Funk

After three years, everything went sour: the Coke sponsorship ran out and the producers started telling me that my on-air voice was too shrill. They said I didn't really fit in with the station and I should probably flip into a research role.

For a while, I was stuck behind a desk, which didn't suit me at all. I kept thinking, "God, I want to be on air!" I liked writing my own stuff and I liked doing interviews. It frustrated me to do all the research and give it to somebody else who, as far as I was concerned, would blow it. But I kept thinking, "If the biggest radio station in the country is telling me I don't have the voice or the style to be on air, they must know what they're talking about. There's simply something wrong with me because I want something I'm not suited for."

It was an interesting lesson to learn. It's like Morales in *A Chorus Line*: she wants to be an actress, and her acting teacher's telling her she can't because she's no good. Finally, she realizes it's not her that's no good, it's the teacher. She's not nothing — he is! A lot of people have to learn that lesson: that somebody in a position of experience and authority may be completely wrong. You just have to find out what you want, push through, and make it happen for yourself.

It was a big stumbling block. Luckily, I was helping one of the announcers, Andy Barrie, as his producer and researcher. He was hugely sympathetic. He would tell me to go report on a story, tape it, write it up, and present it on his show. Occasionally he would get memos from his program director saying, "Don't encourage Valerie." But he was very helpful and supportive.

And then I did the classic "kid thing" and approached my senior colleagues, asking them what to do. I would take people like Betty Kennedy and Gordon Sinclair out for lunch and ask their advice. "If they got complaints about your voice," someone told me, "you should work on your voice."

It was a good idea. I called one of my old drama teachers from high school, met with her, and asked how I could make my voice less high pitched. Was I too tense? Too nervous? What was making my voice rise up? We had two or three meetings where we did a few exercises like slowly reciting poems by

Shelley. "I am Ozymandias, King of Kings. Look upon my works, ye Mighty, and despaaaaiiiir!"

Anyway, the program director heard about these little meetings and thought it was impressive that I was trying. And then my career just turned. I don't know why. I could never really explain it. All of a sudden I became "okay." When Andy Barrie or Betty Kennedy would go on vacation, it was now all right for me to fill in.

Every Pringle Moment

I still had to get past the perception that I was a leftover summer student. They obviously liked me and they had kept me there, but it was hard to be taken seriously. Sometimes I'd think about getting a job somewhere else, so I could enter at an adult level. I'd be in my mid-twenties and people would finally take me a little seriously.

Valerie Pringle: "I was almost apoplectic with fear about having my own show."

I went and saw two or three program directors at other stations. People kept saying, "If you've worked at CFRB, you can get a job anywhere." I made a few little forays, but I never heard back: people weren't exactly beating a path to my door. I wasn't the most focused or ambitious person in that domain. I wasn't desperate to be successful or to have some great career. I was content to keep working.

Luckily, through a bit of patience and persistence, it all paid off. I had my first child at twenty-seven, and when I came back from maternity leave, Andy Barrie decided to move to another station. What really floored me was when they gave me his old job. That was a shock. Only a year before, I was still "shrill-queen." It was a sign that made everything click. They'd shown faith in me. They didn't think I'd screw up. Everything became more serious from my point of view, so I had to work a lot harder to prove myself.

They gave me an hour-long daytime show called *The Pringle Program*. The ad said, "Every Pringle moment is terrific." It was great but terrifying. I was almost apoplectic with fear about having my own show. Andy Barrie had been so good, and I didn't think I could live up to that. It's interesting, all those fears you have — that you're not going to survive the week, let alone the month or the year — you somehow get through them.

Television

I was loving radio. After a couple years of *The Pringle Program*, the television opportunities started to pop up. I was loath to take them at that point because I liked where I was. I was always offended when people assumed that you had to graduate from radio to TV — that TV was implicitly better. "I can make a career in radio," I thought. "Radio is perfectly good. It's not like going from the Brownies to the Girl Guides."

I still think the best broadcasters come from radio. When you're in radio, unless you're reading a news script, you just have to talk. Most people on radio have to find their own speaking voice, their own cadence, their own way of communicating, and their own interviewing style. Many people on TV simply mimic other announcers. It's gotten looser with twenty-four-hour TV and all the MuchMusic stuff, but certainly in the days when I was starting to broadcast, if you came out of the news side, you had a news tone. And if you were a woman in the news you had to have a very tough, ballsy delivery, supposedly for credibility or something.

One day, I was approached by some people from the CBC. They told me they were putting together a new program that would be called *Midday*. They were looking for hosts and my name had been suggested to the producer. It was interesting that they were reaching a broader pool outside the CBC and actually getting someone from private radio — because there usually wasn't much crossover. Nevertheless, I was called, I auditioned, and I got the job.

As a TV co-host, I didn't want to start talking in a weird, mannered

---

I am a child of the Depression. I would have loved to go to university, but my family couldn't afford it. After finishing Grade 11, I had to find my own way to attend secretarial college. I then worked as a secretary until Canadian Kellogg promoted me to office manager and moved me from Montreal to Toronto. Until that point, all the rest of the office management at the company was male. It was a tough go, but I succeeded through hard work and by ensuring that people had confidence in my abilities.

Too few women today feel comfortable demonstrating confidence. They feel their role is to be weak. I have succeeded in the public and private sectors because I have been confident in myself and because I have instilled confidence in others. For a woman to be successful, she has to act like a lady and work like a dog.

— **Hazel McCallion**, Mayor of Mississauga, Ontario, who has served for eleven terms and kept the city debt-free for more than twenty years way. I had developed my own unique voice from radio. A lot of people have critiqued me over the years, saying, "You're just perky," or "You shouldn't laugh on TV." Sometimes I was serious if things were serious, but if they weren't, I wasn't going to pretend to be serious. You've got to have range. Life is full of range. It gets sad and then it gets funny and then it gets silly. I wanted to talk more like a human being.

I grew to love TV. Every once in a while, as I get old, I think maybe radio would be a better place. Especially if I'm shooting a series in high definition and I'm scared about how wrinkly I might look. But I'll worry about that later.

Changes

I think it has become harder to find entry-level jobs. I don't hear about many internships or places that will hire kids. The CBC has cut back and they only hire a few. I think CTV takes on a few interns for smaller jobs, but I don't think they get to be on air. When young people ask what they should do, it's problematic because you don't want to sound discouraging. In some ways, budgets have shrunk and everything's smaller. I still believe that bright, talented young people will succeed and are recognized quite quickly. If you're good at it, you get identified and you move up.

I don't know how I planned it. There's no great intelligence involved, and not much advice, but I probably picked the perfect thing for me to do. I'm always saying to my own kids, "Don't panic. It takes a long time to learn what you want to do. So many people don't find their passion until later on. Don't worry that you don't know when you're at school, or when you just graduated, or five years after graduating."

My brother and sisters had a much harder time of it. Most people do. But for me, I studied radio and television when I was seventeen years old. I got my first job in radio at nineteen. I was married and working full-time when I was twenty. I've been doing this for over thirty-one years now and it's still the best job for me. It suits me. I'd be the worst lawyer. I'd be the worst banker. I hate meetings. I'm incompetent in so many ways. So it was good to find something that I was actually good at. I was really lucky.

"If you don't love what you're doing, you'll never be wholly successful."

In the Vancouver area, **Jim Pattison** is a virtual superstar. The self-made billionaire sits alone atop Canada's third largest privately held company, the Jim Pattison Group. He owns the advertising signs commuters pass on their way to work, a large chunk of the Western Canadian retail food industry, and sixty-two *Ripley's Believe It or Not!* attractions across the globe. He was also the CEO and chairman of Vancouver's world exhibition, Expo '86. Though today he lives in Frank Sinatra's old Palm Springs mansion, Pattison got off to a modest start, selling cars on the campus of the University of British Columbia. When asked for the secret to his success, Pattison offers a confounded shrug that clearly indicates he is rarely paralyzed by indecision. He just went out and made money.

The son of a car salesman who lost his livelihood during the Depression, Pattison grew up hawking everything from newspapers and magazine subscriptions to garden seeds and adhesive tape. The lean years when his father was forced to de-moth pianos door to door taught Pattison a valuable lesson: work hard and always look ahead.

Earning Trust

Often, salesmanship can be seen as a slimy business where you lie and distort to get ahead. That may work for some people, but what customers really respond to is honesty.

Growing up as an only child, my mother and father were my whole life. In terms of role models, I had the two of them and the local minister. My parents were fairly religious people; we worked every week at a skid row mission in downtown Vancouver. The minister was a highly principled man who taught me never to lie, cheat, or steal.

The values instilled at home and at the mission have stayed with me to this day. They have also helped me in business. If you're honest and hard-working, even in the face of adversity, people will respond positively to what you're selling.

University: A Means to an End

While I was enrolled in the arts and commerce program at the University of British Columbia, I worked a number of jobs. I was a pantry man in a railway dining car and later I washed cars at a local auto dealer. Gradually, I saw an opportunity for myself. I realized that a number of students were looking for used cars and there was no place to buy them on campus.

Jim Pattison: "I realized that a number of students were looking for used cars and there was no place to buy them on campus."

Sensing an opportunity, I went through the classifieds and found good deals on cars. I would buy a car, fix it up, drive it onto campus, hike the price up by a small margin — say $25 or $50 — sell it, and either take the bus home or get a ride with a friend.

After my third year, I realized I was getting good at selling, so I went down to Kingsway, the street in Vancouver where all the big used car dealers were, and found an empty lot. I got it into my head that I could sell cars on the lot while I finished my final year of school. When I approached the landlord, he informed me the Nash dealer had leased the lot the day before. "But he's looking for someone to run it," the landlord said. "He might hire you."

I approached the Nash dealer, Dan McLean, and told him I wanted to run the lot for him. Luckily for me, my father had worked for him several years earlier, during which time he had built up a good reputation for himself. Dan knew my dad was honest and he figured I was too. He gave me the job on the spot.

It was impossible to keep up with my courses and work at the same time, so I dropped out of university. Later on, though, Dan allowed me to go back to school and take some courses so I could finish my degree. However, I left UBC nine units short of graduating.

Setting Benchmarks

At the time, I had no massive career plan. I just took things a day at a time. As a sales manager, I set targets for myself. To this day, I continue to do so.

After a while, Dan bought a General Motors dealership and took me on to manage the used car side of the business. As time went on, I became the new car manager and then the general manager of the dealership. I stayed there for ten years.

Doing What You Enjoy

As a general manager, I was earning $6,000 a year. One day, a customer came into the dealership and mentioned that he needed someone to run his pots and pans business. He said the position paid $50,000 a year. I loved selling cars, but the offer seemed too good to resist. I accepted and sold pots and pans for a year. It taught me a valuable lesson: simply making money isn't enough. To be happy, you need to have a passion for what you do. By the end of the year, I went back to the dealership.

As a manager, I concentrated on raising the quality of our salespeople. That belief sprang from experience. Typically, I found that the people at the bottom weren't performing because they weren't working hard or they weren't cut out to be salespeople. What's the point of keeping them around if they're not doing the company any good and they aren't doing what they love?

If you don't love what you're doing, you'll never be wholly successful. You may do okay for a while — you may be competent — but if you don't love what you're doing, then you won't be able to go the extra mile.

The Importance of Being Focused

In many ways, it was easier for me than it is for young people today. I had no distractions. Today, there are a seemingly unlimited number of distractions. Some young people struggle to keep their focus. But focus is essential. If you're focused on what you want, and you're not lying to yourself, then you'll be fine. You can't chase after a thousand things at once. Find one thing that you want and pursue it.

Through my twenties, I never worried about the direction of my career. I only concerned myself with being able to make my next project. I still function the same way today. To a filmmaker, "success" is when you don't have to suffer the pain of running around to raise money. When — and if — that moment ever comes, you are successful. Otherwise, you just worry about getting the next film made.

— **Deepa Mehta**, Academy Award–nominated director of *Water*

*"Once you see your first book on the shelf,
you say to yourself, 'This is just the beginning.'"*

Lynn Johnston is the creator of the internationally syndicated comic *For Better or Worse*. Since first appearing in 1979, the semi-autobiographical strip, which follows the ongoing tribulations of the Patterson family, has made waves for its warm, comic realism and its tackling of hot-button social issues. It has even been adapted into a successful animated TV series on three separate occasions. In 1985, Johnston became the first woman and the first Canadian to win the prestigious Reuben Award for Outstanding Cartoonist.

Lynn Johnston grew up addicted to comic books. "Nowadays, people live through the fantasy world of their Xboxes," she says. "Back then, without television, all the kids had comics, which we collected and traded." Johnston wanted to be an animator, doodling in class, making flip-books, and writing comics about the love lives of her teachers. As she got older, however, the idea of being a professional animator seemed less and less realistic. As a compromise, Johnston opted to study commercial art at the Vancouver School of Art.

Art School Woes

When I got to the Vancouver School of Art, the equipment and teaching methods were fifteen years out of date. Even though newspapers and magazines had started using colour and cutting-edge advertising agencies were using new printing techniques, we were forced to work in black and white and do all our lettering by hand. I've always been very outspoken. Since we weren't allowed to be progressive, I clowned around at the teachers' expense and wasn't very popular with them as a result.

During third year, my father found me a job in the ink and paint department at a company called Canawest. We were contracted by an American television station that had taken on work in Vancouver because of low Canadian wages. The two cartoons we worked on were *Shazam* and *Abbott and Costello*. I was one of sixteen girls in the ink and paint department. We worked shoulder to shoulder, painting cells and producing absolute garbage. After I had been at Canawest for a while, I started to apprentice under the company's head animator. We worked together on commercials and he taught me how to storyboard a scene. He could see that I desperately wanted to become an animator.

Lynn Johnston: "When you excel at something and work at it long enough, your experience becomes your diploma."

Going from art school, where everything was out of date, to a modern animation studio was amazing. I knew I'd never go back to school. I later regretted never getting my "piece of paper," but when you excel at something and work at it long enough, your experience becomes your diploma.

Married Too Soon

When I was twenty I got married to a CBC cameraman. My brother used to say, "The only reason you got married was to get out of the house." It really upset me at the time, but he was right. I married the wrong person at the wrong time and for the wrong reasons. I realized it much later — when it was too late.

After we were married, we went to Los Angeles to find work. A girl from Canawest had parents who wrote for Walt Disney and they set me up with an interview at J. Ward Studios, the people behind *George of the Jungle*, *Gerald McBoing-Boing*, and all the Captain Crunch commercials. J. Ward offered me a job drawing backgrounds and I was desperate to take it. In those days, there were no animation schools. The only way you could learn was on the job. My husband nixed the idea. His job-hunting had proven unsuccessful, so there was no arguing with him: we were headed back to Canada. That's what you did in those days: you followed your man.

Since jobs in television were increasingly scarce in Vancouver, we eventually moved to Hamilton, Ontario. They assigned me to work on a kids' show called

Rocket Robin Hood, but my animation skills weren't up to snuff. So I took a job as a graphic artist at the Hamilton General Hospital.

Bridging Animation and Health Science

From the very beginning, the head of the photo department and I didn't get along. I had been hired to make drawings for medical texts and films. I discovered that our equipment allowed us to do animation and I wanted to try sequential animated films. The doctors began asking if I could show the various steps of a kidney biopsy and other easy-to-animate procedures. When I began putting in extra hours to give the doctors what they asked for, I was fired. Apparently, I wasn't doing what I had been hired to do.

Luckily, two of the doctors helped me get a job doing medical illustration at McMaster University. I began drawing anatomical and surgical illustrations. It was remarkable work. Doing surgical work taught me to look at the human body more carefully. I was learning to draw in three dimensions. I apply what I learned there every time I draw.

One of the profs I worked with at McMaster was teaching epidemiology and biostatistics. Needless to say, it was fairly tedious stuff — all math, charts, and graphs. Dr. Dave Sackett, head of the department and the son of an editorial cartoonist, asked one day if I could make comic art out of his lecture material. He was doing studies with rats, directing electrodes through different parts of the brain. In one experiment, the rats would be stimulated sexually and in others they were stimulated by hunger. That was easy to draw. I drew one rat, looking like Oil Can Harry, staring at another, who looked like Mae West. Then I drew a third rat, staring at a midnight buffet. I bordered the illustration with data so it was more fun for students while they were studying.

Some of the teaching staff were angry. "Comic art has no place in med school!" they'd say. Dave intervened. "Let's do an experiment," he suggested. "We'll do both," he said. "Let's create pure data slides and art slides, and see which the students respond most favourably to." Predictably, the students remembered the data on my slides more than the others. After that, I was able to devote myself almost entirely to comic art.

Running into Trouble

Things weren't good at home. My marriage was falling apart. One day, I decided to run away and took off to Vancouver without telling anyone. I didn't even phone in to work.

Upon my return, the job at McMaster was — understandably — no longer available. I had to make my own career. I was confident enough to do freelance work, so I set up a studio in the greenhouse behind our house. I froze in the winter and died of heat in the summer, but there was a lot of light and my clientele grew.

David, We're Pregnant

When I was pregnant with my first child, I did roughly eighty drawings about the experience of childbirth on my doctor's ceiling. A few months later, he called me to his house and said he thought we could make them into a book. He even helped find a publisher. That work on his ceiling was a large part of what became my first book of comics, *David, We're Pregnant*.

When our son was six months old, my husband abandoned us. Suddenly, I had to get full-time work to pay the bills. I knew some artists in town and they managed to get me a job with Standard Engravers, a packaging company that made boxes for everything from pharmaceuticals to farm materials. I did puzzles on the backs of cereal boxes and drawings showing how to keep bugs out of your hayfield. "We've got a four-inch square on this box," they would say. "What can you do?" That space was mine. It was like having a tiny corner of the job to myself.

Having gone from doing billboards, comic art, and big posters in my own studio, it was a real adjustment to be doing black and white illustrations at an industrial job. But it was the best thing that could have happened. I learned all about print type, photography, ruby liths, and everything that goes into putting a magazine together.

Soon after the book came out, I left Standard Engravers and went back to freelancing. But the publisher

I grew up in a large family in Nigeria. When I immigrated to Canada, I was suddenly alone and it was freezing cold outside. I had no means of financial support and everyone called me "dude" (which, at the time, I thought was an insult). I went on welfare for the first half-year, but the $400 a month evaporated soon after paying for my food, my transportation, my gym memberships, and my rent. I kept thinking, "Wow, I didn't have it so bad in Nigeria. At least there, the state covered my expenses."

I just kept reminding myself why I was here: I knew the Canadian system would make me a better wrestler and that a Canadian degree would open doors for me. As a result, I did everything I could to keep afloat. While attending Simon Fraser University and training with their wrestling team, I worked as a security guard from 11:00 p.m. to 7:00 a.m. Staying awake in class was difficult, but I pressed on. Later, I pumped gas, picked berries, did some babysitting, and worked at kids' camps. I put my personal life on hold, kept my head in the classroom, and focused on improving my athletic performance.

—**Daniel Igali**, wrestler, gold medallist in the Sydney Olympics, and Canada's Athlete of the Year in 2000 was unable to pay me the royalties and I was forced to go on welfare. After I paid the mortgage, hydro, heat, and everything, there was only $20 a week for groceries. My ex-husband had always been the one who took care of the finances and the paperwork. Suddenly, I had to learn about being a responsible adult, with everything on the line.

At first, I lived on nothing. Slowly, as the book started to sell — and freelance jobs increased — I was able to get by as I worked on the second book. Once you see your first book on the shelf, you say to yourself, "This is just the beginning." There's no way you're going to let it sit by itself. Plus, you know the second one will help sell the first.

Getting It Together

When I started seeing Rod, my second husband, I gradually managed to get things back on track. We moved in together and were married fairly quickly. Because he was in dental school, we didn't have much money coming in. I did as much freelance as I could — mixing medical art, commercial art, and comic art. We'd rent out our house in the summertime and go to work on his sister's farm.

The problem was that the second book didn't make much money either. The publisher was also unable to pay me.

Universal Press

A lot of your success comes from the work you put into your endeavours. But so much comes from the support of others. I've found that, throughout my life, there's always been someone with contacts who had faith in me. Their support gave me confidence and made me work that little bit harder. When someone helps you out, you want to exceed their expectations.

That's what happened with my third book. I found an American publisher from Minneapolis. He was so excited about my drawings that he passed them on to the Universal Press Syndicate. "If you don't syndicate her," he told them, "I will." On his recommendation, Universal Press Syndicate wrote me, asking if I was interested in doing a daily comic strip. It caught me completely by surprise. They wanted twenty cartoons as fast as possible. They wanted to see how fast I could produce. They'd seen my work, but they didn't know how long it had taken me to do. When you're syndicated, you have to be able to hit a deadline every month and remain six to eight weeks ahead of the publishing date. Plus, when you're new, they edit you like crazy, so they needed to know that I could produce quality on demand.

I hurriedly put together twenty comics, never expecting to hear from UPS again. I called the strip "The Johnstons." The whole thing was based on my family, because they were the only people I could consistently draw over and over again. When Universal Press offered me a contract, I was shocked. Full-time work for a cartoonist is virtually unheard of.

Support from the Community

I didn't know what to do. I desperately needed advice. I'd read comics my whole life, but I'd never met a syndicated artist. I called Cathy Guisewite, the creator of *Cathy*, and asked her how she worked and what she'd learned. She was very eager to help. Because it's such a unique business, everyone is open to talking about their tricks and habits.

I ultimately found a huge support system in the comic community. It's like a fraternity of people, all of whom are intensely self-critical. Finding that community was such a gift. It made adapting to the pace and pressure of doing syndicated comics much easier.

BEVERLEY McLACHLIN

"Most of what you learn about life, they say, is learned before you're thirty."

Living on her family's cattle ranch, **Beverley McLachlin**, a self-described "farm girl," was instilled with a strong work ethic at an early age. It was in the town of Pincher Creek, Alberta, a community of varied religious groups and mixed social classes, that she developed the tolerance and egalitarianism she still holds today. As chief justice of the Supreme Court of Canada, she has been integral in nearly every important judicial decision of the last decade: upholding the constitutionality of swingers' clubs, allowing for private medical insurance in Quebec, and striking down severe anti-terrorism laws.

A long-time lover of reading and writing, she originally contemplated a career in journalism. Before long, however, she became immersed in the study of law and interested specifically in the philosophical underpinnings of legal theory. After graduating, she worked for firms in Edmonton and Vancouver before accepting a teaching position at the University of British Columbia. Appointed as a provincial judge in 1981, she joined the country's highest court eight years later and, in 2000, was named chief justice, the first woman in Canada to hold the position.

Choosing Law

I thought about becoming a writer. I toyed with journalism, working a little at the University of Alberta's *Gateway* and taking a summer job at a newspaper. It was an interesting time to be writing in the province, in the last years of Ernest Manning's Social Credit government, as it moved from a traditional agricultural society to a more diverse one.

I toyed with three possible careers: having decided against journalism, I then thought I'd do graduate work and teach philosophy; finally, I decided upon a law degree. Ultimately, I chose law because I needed something a little more hands-on. I liked the idea of meeting real people and trying to work with them.

I stayed at the University of Alberta for my law degree, taking courses during the summer that eventually led to a master's in the philosophy of law. As a result, I never had any jobs — either with a firm or otherwise — while at law school. Additionally, I applied for and received a generous bursary, allowing me to spend my last summer developing my thesis.

My work centred on the links between philosophy and law. There is a lot of overlap. When you study philosophy, you study legal systems. You start with Socrates' and Plato's reflections on law and justice, then work your way to the present, law being integral all along. Through philosophy, I adopted a new outlook on the world — derived from the ancient Greeks — of working out a coherent, logical argument for both sides of an issue. I learned to think critically, to get my thoughts straight and to put them on paper in a defensible way.

However, I soon found that no matter what job you have, it's important to understand why you're doing it and what value it has for society. For me, there's never been a distinction between philosophical theories and day-to-day living: if you're a mother, you should have a "philosophy" about being a good mother.

Moving On

In my last year at school, I had an interview with an Edmonton firm for an articling position. Even though I was enthusiastic about working for them — and the interview went well — I didn't hear back for a number of weeks. It worried me a great deal, so I decided to phone them up. When I finally got through to the recruitment agent, he didn't seem to be very troubled. "Of course you're hired," he said. "We've discussed it and you were selected." The experience taught me that young people often have to be a little courageous to get what they're after, instead of

Should I have practised law longer before starting my political career at the age of twenty-four? I've rerun that question many times. Would it have been useful or interesting to have some years at the bar before becoming involved politically? Yes, I think it would have been. At the same time, if I had worked in law, I might have become less likely to give politics a try. As in any career, you get your roots down, you get well established, and you get a partnership. It can become difficult to disengage.

—**Ralph Goodale**, federal minister of finance, 2003–06, Liberal Member of Parliament for Wascana (pictured with Pierre Trudeau)

Beverley McLachlin: "For me, there's never been a distinction between philosophical theories and day-to-day living."

waiting by the phone for that breakthrough call. I was annoyed they hadn't contacted me themselves, but I couldn't complain: I was glad to be employed.

My practical education really began after I started to article. I was given the chance to do a little bit of everything at work. I was even able to go to court and defend people on charges.

Though it may have been difficult for other women in the legal world at the time, I had great support in the firm. People were always willing to look at the quality of the work I did and not write me off because I was the wrong gender. I was lucky. Women were regarded as something of an oddity, so you had to be prepared to live with the occasional negative comment. These days, there's more acceptance of women in the professional field. There are, however, still many challenges.

The trick is simply to be as good as you can be and to enjoy it. I think the practice of law is very different now. It's become bigger and more commercialized. Back then, practising law was a lot of fun in the sense that you were not as worried. Many young people I talk to now are stressed about the hours they've billed. That just wasn't a part of my life. But the world changes.

The West Coast

My husband was working in British Columbia, so I followed him to Vancouver and learned to love another wonderful city. It was a different kind of society, but one that was very open. With good references and a contact from a friend in Edmonton, I was able to get a job at a big firm where I became more involved in large-scale litigation. The legal culture in British Columbia was very dynamic. There was a lot of excitement, and people were willing to take on all sorts of different cases: commercial, civil liberties, Aboriginal issues. I enjoyed it very much.

It's important to remember that to get a job in the legal world, the relationships you make along the way are important. I was always lucky because I was able to form good relationships with the people I worked with. They were very concerned to help me along when I needed it, which made a big difference when I was on my own in a new city.

That's what happened when, after a few years of practice, I was asked to teach a part-time course in civil litigation at the University of British Columbia. I really enjoyed the material and the students. I thought I might like to fully cross over to the academic world for a while, so I became a full-time professor for nearly six years. Afterwards, I would have gone back into practice, but I was asked to go on the bench at the County Court of Vancouver. So I took that instead.

Lessons

Most of what you learn about life, they say, is learned before you're thirty. I realized that success was never just a career matter. Balance was very important. I've been fortunate because I've always been able to balance my career with other interests. You have to train yourself to get away for periods of time, whether it's a weekend at the cottage, a day in the garden, or a few hours on a lake. In Vancouver, before I had a place in the country, we used to go down to the Gulf Islands. I always loved being outdoors and taking long walks.

Success is also about living up to the best in yourself and contributing to the community. If you can leave the world a slightly better place, if you can help improve people's lives and realize more or less such talents as God has given you, then you've been successful.

PATRICK MORROW

*"In those early years, I was the quintessential dirt-bag photographer.
I had no idea how to make a living at my craft."*

In 1986, **Patrick Morrow** became the first person to climb the "Seven Summits," the highest peaks on each of the world's continents. Morrow's ticket to this life of adventure? His camera. After chronicling the early days of frozen-waterfall climbing in the Canadian Rockies, Morrow went on to shoot expeditions in some of the world's most breathtaking and far-flung locations. Over the past ten years, working alongside his wife, Baiba, he has made the transition to filmmaking, producing consciousness-raising documentaries like *The Magic Mountain*, an award-winning account of former climber Cynthia Hunt's health education programs in Ladakh.

Morrow grew up in Kimberley, a mining town in southeastern British Columbia. The Rockies and the Purcell Range were his backyard. He could access countless snowshoeing paths from the end of his street. School work was of little interest to Morrow, until he discovered the nature-oriented poems of Wordsworth and Keats and, later, a small volume of Ernest Hemingway's reports from the Spanish Civil War. Around the same time, he was introduced to technical rock climbing and vowed to make mountaineering a central part of his life. To do so was a major challenge. In the end, a love for storytelling and high adventure became the two sides of a lifelong passion.

White Wilderness

When I was a teenager, rock climbing hadn't gone mainstream yet. Nowadays, there are climbers living in virtually every mountain town in Western Canada, but in the 1960s, there were only a handful in the interior of B.C. As a result, I had to rely on my high school buddies as rope partners and learn as much as I could from books.

Over time, I was influenced by the philosophical approach to climbing taken by authors like Lionel Terray and Reinhold Messner. These world-renowned mountaineers portrayed climbing to be as much a spiritual pursuit as a physical one. Messner coined the term "White Wilderness," a call for policy-makers to work toward the continued existence of unspoiled white spaces on the map. The more I climbed and the more first-hand experiences I built up, the more I believed in their philosophies.

Finding Photography

Climbing quickly emerged as my first love, but, upon discovering the visceral style of Ernest Hemingway's non-fiction, journalism pointed the way to a future vocation. At sixteen, I decided to submit a piece to the local newspaper. It was a story on one of the first snowmobile races in the area. I slaved away on the piece, hoping to blow the editors away and force them to hire me. The moment of reckoning came when the editor judiciously chopped my multi-page story down to a few lines and ran my accompanying photo large. Suddenly, a little light blinked on. It had taken only a fraction of a second to take the photo, yet that's what had moved the editor. From that point on, I knew my camera would get me further than my typewriter. As a result, I began focusing more attention on improving my photography.

I spent the next year taking photographs for the newspaper on a freelance basis. Luckily for me, during the same period, an American photographer named Art Twomey moved to a log cabin that he built up in the Purcell Range. He used his still and film cameras to help create the Purcell Wilderness Conservancy, the first of its kind in British Columbia. His lifestyle and photography called out to me, solidifying my belief that photographs of the wild could be used to galvanize efforts to protect it.

Struggling to Find a Subject

At seventeen, I moved to Calgary to study journalism at the Southern Alberta Institute of Technology. The program taught us how to run a local newspaper. I was disappointed at the time that the course didn't focus on photojournalism, but in retrospect, it gave me a solid overview of how media outlets worked.

Midway through my second year, I left to become a photography intern at the *Calgary Herald*. For the first month, I tagged along alternately with the paper's seven staff photographers. I did everything from covering late-night traffic accidents to taking portraits of visiting dignitaries. While this was interesting at first, the daily grind burnt me out. There are only so many ways you can shoot a news or sporting event, and I found the frantic deadlines counterproductive. I realized I needed to forge a different path — one where I earned a living photographing subjects of my own choice and following my own schedule.

To do that, I needed to learn about the more technical aspects of the art, so I enrolled in the now-defunct photography program at the Banff Centre. That was the best course I have ever taken. The program's director, Bob Alexander, structured it so we received a lecture and an assignment on Monday and reconvened every Friday for assessment by instructors and fellow students. Since it was a general arts school, we had exposure to all kinds of artists and performers, which helped shape and challenge our points of view.

At the time, I was drawn to the newly developed winter sport of frozen-waterfall climbing, where people would ascend near-vertical ice formations created by waterfalls. I spent two winters freezing my buns off at temperatures down to -30°C, climbing and photographing some very talented climbers from the Calgary and Banff areas. At first, I was drawn to the challenge and thrill of making an ascent on steep ice, but soon it occurred to me that the sport provided remarkable visuals that the publishing world needed to see. Those photos would eventually appear in a multi-page spread in a small American climbing magazine called *Summit*, which helped kick off my career, as well as the sport itself. Soon after it appeared, a wave of climbers from the United States flooded northwards to start ticking first ascents (much to the chagrin of local climbers).

Surviving as a Freelancer

The climbers I met during those two winters taught me a valuable lesson on how to survive as a freelancer. They were mostly working-class Brits who pounded nails in and around Calgary and Banff for a couple of months and then used everything they made to travel the world for a year or more. Their mantra was "keep your overhead down."

In those early years, I was the quintessential dirt-bag photographer. I had no idea how to make a living at my craft. All I knew was that I was happy, so I kept soldiering on, convinced that things would eventually come together. Luckily, my father offered me free rent in Kimberley during this period. Without his generosity, I would never have been able to afford gas for my van or the expensive rolls of Kodachrome for my camera.

When I graduated from Banff in 1975, a friend suggested I visit the photo marketplace, which is primarily in the east. I invested in a thirty-day Greyhound excursion ticket, and crashed on friends' floors in Toronto, Montreal, Ottawa,

New York, and Washington, D.C. Upon returning, I was armed with contacts, buoyed by positive feedback from the magazine pros, and inspired by the wonderful things I'd seen in the galleries of New York. I had more than enough fuel to stay energized and busy.

Patrick Morrow: "I've always been driven by curiosity rather than artistic perfection."

Before the Internet, it was incredibly difficult to promote yourself and get your work into editors' hands. Unless your photographs and writing were already published, it was unlikely that editors would catch wind of you. Meeting those editors in person and maintaining long-term contact was essential.

Adventure Journalism

I've always been driven by curiosity rather than artistic perfection. Some photographers I know are anal about their work. To them, the only thing that matters is what the shots look like. They seem to derive little pleasure from the life experiences that radiate out of each assignment. For me, it's the opposite. Of course my photographs need to be good — otherwise they'll never sell. But I put a much higher value on the life lessons that come as a result of what my camera has allowed me to do.

I was inspired by American adventurer Ned Gillette. Throughout the 1970s, he and photographer Galen Rowell engaged in some of the more innovative climbing and skiing projects chronicled at the time. Ned was a former member of the U.S. cross-country ski team. Unlike 99 percent of professionally trained athletes, he actually did something interesting in the adventure world once he retired, writing a book and numerous magazine stories on journeys he'd taken to some of the most remote peaks. I admired the way he underplayed his accomplishments, communicating instead the importance of seeking out challenges beyond one's comfort level.

Opportunities of a Lifetime

One of the first big trips I took was to climb Mt. Denali, the highest peak in North America. In the spring of 1977, I drove to Alaska in a VW Bug with my friend Bernhard Ehmann, hoping to establish a new route to the summit. One of the climbers in our group was Roger Marshall of Golden, B.C. The next year, Roger applied for and received a permit to climb Mt. Everest in 1982. It was going to be the first Canadian expedition on the world's highest mountain. Roger had seen my photos of the Denali climb published in the *Canadian Alpine Journal*. Since he wanted to put together a book on the Everest ascent, he invited me on board as the official expedition photographer.

It was the opportunity of a lifetime. I had never had a desire to climb Everest, but how could I possibly turn down the offer? As part of a sponsorship package, Air Canada offered the team plane tickets to two peaks of our choice. The first expedition was in 1981, to a newly opened area in western China. We embarked on a six-week outing to Xinjiang province, through an area few foreigners had travelled since the onset of Communism. We climbed the 7,500-metre peak of Mt. Muztagata in the Pamir range and were the fourth team to ever reach the top. Skiing right off the summit, we carved turns through 3,000 vertical metres of perfect powder to the base, and then spent two dreamlike days skiing the 300-metre-high sand dunes near the foot of the mountain. One of my photos from that trip landed on the cover of the inaugural issue of *Equinox* magazine, along with a generous spread inside. That story kick-started my international career in adventure journalism. My photos from China also appeared in many foreign publications.

A Mixed Experience

The Everest expedition itself was ultimately a tragic one. Roger Marshall, the original organizer, was booted from the team before we got to the mountain. Three Sherpas and Canadian cameraman Blair Griffiths died in the Khumbu Icefall, which prompted half our team to abandon the expedition.

Obviously, for me, as a twenty-nine-year-old photographer at the height of my game, all the ups and heartbreaking downs of the expedition provided fodder for my camera. And when Blair died, I picked up his video camera in an effort to document the remainder of the climb.

On summit day, October 7, 1982, the video camera battery died, but both of my small SLR cameras kept working. I photographed my two Sherpa partners as I roped them up to me over the crux of the climb, the ten-metre-high Hillary Step, and we embraced on the summit.

When I stopped to change a roll of film just below the summit, I got my only frostbite of the expedition, on my fingertips. In the frigid air, the film kept breaking off, until finally I got it loaded. The experience I had accumulated from all those years of winter ascents in the Rockies, and various other far-off adventures, paid off.

A Desk Job

People often ask if I could ever be content with a desk job. What they don't understand is that I have one of the most arduous desk jobs around. Even though I'm off on photographic or filmmaking junkets for large chunks at a time, the six sporadic months when I'm at home, I'm chained to my desk. As a freelancer, with no guaranteed income, your only security is to spend twelve hours a day in the office, trying to keep several projects in the air at once.

The hidden world of the freelancer is in no way glamorous, but it's allowed me to live a life with few physical boundaries. I've stood at both the North and South Poles, the apex of the world, and endless photographic high points in between — all in the pursuit of adventure.

"Maybe I could contribute by changing people's attitudes."

Rick Hansen always loved sports and the outdoors. During his early adolescence in Williams Lake, British Columbia, his goal was to represent Canada on the national volleyball team, followed by a career as a phys-ed teacher. That all changed when he was fifteen. While hitchhiking back from a fishing trip, he got into a car accident and was paralyzed from the waist down by a spinal cord injury. After a lengthy rehabilitation process, he soon realized he would have to spend the rest of his life in a wheel-chair.

Setbacks never stopped him for very long. Hansen has become a renowned wheelchair athlete, picking up several medals at the Paralympic Games and even competing in the 1984 Los Angeles Olympics. He is best known for pushing himself across the globe during his Man in Motion World Tour, a forty-thousand-kilometre trek inspired by his late friend Terry Fox. The tour raised $26 million for spinal cord research.

Coping with Disability

Immediately after my accident, I went through a period of denial. First of all, I believed I'd recover. I had sprained my ankle before and I had friends who had broken bones, and I thought it would get better. But I was about to realize — with a broken back — that the central nervous system is complex and all the willpower in the world can't overcome an injury like that. When friends or my coach would visit, I'd be speaking positively about joining the team again in six months' time. But after four or five months at the GF Strong Rehabilitation Centre, I began to realize that this was serious. I didn't have any improvement in the nerve or muscle recovery of my legs. I began to consider that my life as an athlete and an outdoorsman might be over. That was tough. It wasn't until I got home months later that I started reframing the future possibilities for my life.

When I finally returned home, there were a number of people who encouraged me. One of them was Bob Redford, my volleyball coach and high school phys-ed teacher. He was a great guy who extended himself to get me back into the gym. After facing some initial challenges, I realized that I still loved sports — that's where my friends were and that's where my life was.

Soon Bob was introducing me to wheelchair sports. He showed me that the definition of athleticism had nothing to do with whether I could move my legs or not. I soon saw that wheelchair sports were highly competitive and well developed. I could sit in my chair and do almost anything, propelling myself by my arms instead of my legs — and being driven by my heart.

Rick Hansen: "I could sit in my chair and do almost anything, propelling myself by my arms instead of my legs — and being driven by my heart."

That was a pretty pivotal time. Bob knew that my long-term aspiration was to be a phys-ed teacher and he helped me overcome the stigma that if I couldn't physically demonstrate all the movements then I couldn't teach. He first got me involved in coaching at elementary schools and then at high schools, as well as doing some substitute teaching. He had to bend the rules a little and get my confidence up. Once you see the possibilities, you begin to set goals again.

University

I decided to apply for first-year phys-ed at the University of British Columbia. I was very open about my circumstances in the application letter. They responded by saying they couldn't accept my application at the time. They invited me to come in and take first-year arts and science and then we could talk about the possibilities for year two. I felt like I had been completely rejected.

I considered just staying at home for another year and continuing to coach. But Bob made me see this as an opportunity. Maybe they'd never had anyone in a wheelchair apply before and they weren't sure about the responsibility. They didn't want to make the wrong choice, either for me or for the program. This could be a challenge — to come down and convince them I was the right person. So I did some thinking and agreed to go and do first-year arts and science.

That year went well. I wasn't exactly a studious individual and I didn't do a lot of studying, but I crammed enough to get reasonable marks. I got by with enough to advance and was able to save most of my energy for what I really wanted to do. I was also able to convince them to let me into the phys-ed program.

Wheelchair Basketball and Friendship

By the time I was twenty, I was in my second year of phys-ed and pretty immersed in wheelchair basketball. Before becoming involved, my perception was that wheelchair sports weren't very competitive. Once I started playing and met some of the athletes, I realized that it was *highly* competitive. The North American Wheelchair Basketball Association had over a hundred teams. Being in the top-ranked level was quite an eye-opener for me.

One of my inspirations was a man named Stan Strong. He was one of the first people to survive a spinal cord injury and he was a counsellor for the Paraplegic Association. He was also a manager for wheelchair basketball and was assigned to my team, the Vancouver Cable Cars. At a time when I was feeling sorry for myself, he wheeled into my life with a big grin on his face and made me realize I didn't need to be cured in order to be whole. He exuded life, purpose, and potential. Nobody knows about Stan Strong, but he's an example of what makes the country strong.

He organized and managed the team. He had to mortgage his house to get it going, take us to tournaments, and buy equipment. He was always challenging me to find new recruits. Because of that, I ended up having dinner one night with a friend who told me about this young man who had just lost his leg to cancer and who used to play JV basketball at Simon Fraser University. I got his name and I called him when I got home. His name was Terry Fox.

We spoke and he said he wanted to come and play ball with the Cable Cars. At the time he was struggling with having just lost his leg and wondering what the future would be like. I knew that having him immersed in a competitive environment, with guys who were disabled but so athletic, would inspire and challenge him. I was right: he came to take the sport incredibly seriously.

I was pretty fortunate to have him as a friend. We had a lot in common: we both loved sports and were very competitive, and while I was doing phys-ed courses, he was studying kinesiology at Simon Fraser. We ended up spending a lot of time together. We trained, roomed, and travelled together, and I felt privileged to know him.

The Olympics

Within a couple of years, I had shifted my focus to track and wheelchair marathons. I soon found out that the planning team for the 1984 Los Angeles Olympics was going to introduce wheelchair track as an exhibition event. Having participated in the 1980 Paralympics (where I won gold in the 800-metre), the chance to be one of the first wheelchair athletes at the Olympic Games excited me. It was a big deal in our community.

First you had to represent your province at the nationals, then qualify in the top three in order to go on to the qualifiers in New York. It turned out to be a real challenge because the qualifiers took place three months after I had crashed and dislocated my left shoulder while preparing for a marathon. I had to get the shoulder stabilized and recover in time to make it in the top eight to qualify for Los Angeles. As it turned out, I qualified by about one one-hundredth of a second in eighth position.

You can imagine one of the highlights of my athletic career — in addition to the Paralympic medals — was being able to compete in the Olympics. Just to overcome the obstacles along the road. Again, it was a question of redefining the limitations imposed by others. The danger was in limiting yourself. Would you raise the bar and put your head down and persevere every day with the goal of recovering effectively and quickly? When you get past all that, it's a pretty powerful and emotional moment.

The Man in Motion World Tour

The idea of wheeling myself around the world came as a crazy dream. I was thinking about my life and cross-referencing it with old dreams I'd had when I didn't have my disability. I had always wanted to bicycle around the world with some buddies as part of a great adventure. Could I do it in my chair — if not physically, then maybe I could put my chair in a trailer in the back and everybody would be on their bikes and off we'd go?

There were a number of things that shaped and shifted that dream. Obviously, getting involved with wheelchair marathoning and training at such an elite level made me believe that physically I could do it. Meeting guys like Stan Strong and many others, full of goodwill and understanding, made me want to give something back and contribute my skills and talents.

Travelling the world and representing my country, I noticed the physical and attitudinal barriers that were everywhere. It could be tough just getting into a taxi or a hotel room or an airplane. You travel someplace and the taxis wouldn't even pick you up. Or people would look at you funny and cross to the other side of the street to avoid having to deal with you. There was lots of stuff like that. Maybe I could contribute by changing people's attitudes. Maybe I could do something to help remove barriers from a person's life. Maybe anything was possible. It was time for me to step up. I ended my athletic career at the peak by doing something that had a chance to make a difference.

DREAMERS

Canadians Who Blazed Their Own Trails

"It's tough for young people to imagine, but there used to be a lot of public pressure to write happy and supportive stories."

A crusader for social justice and a witty spitfire, **June Callwood** has been called "the conscience of Canada." When she passed away in 2007 at the age of eighty-two, Callwood left an undeniable legacy of integrity and caring. She founded more than fifty social organizations, including Nellie's Women's Shelter, PEN Canada, and Casey House, the country's first AIDS hospice. Her interest in advocacy grew out of her journalism. Despite having no formal education past the age of sixteen, she became one of the most prolific and respected magazine writers in Canada, as well as the host of CBC-TV's *In Touch*. She is the author of twelve books and the ghostwriter of autobiographies by the likes of Barbara Walters and Otto Preminger.

When we met her, June knew that she was sick. Nevertheless, the eighty-two-year-old bounded across Toronto's bustling Yonge Street like a teenager, all smiles and vigour. Throughout the interview, Callwood exuded a bewitching mix of maternal love, unparalleled candour, and biting humour. Her story proves what can be done when we dare to combine nerve and unrelenting integrity.

An Early Calling

My generation was the polar opposite of the one you see entering the workforce today. Now people have all the education they could ever ask for, but they can't commit to a career. In my day, we had no education, but we were totally committed to what we were doing.

I left high school when I was sixteen. My father was a sergeant in the army. Because he was a non-commissioned officer, the family didn't receive much money. I was a bit of a pain in my mother's backside back then, so one day she turned to me and said, "I'm tired of supporting you. Go out and find yourself a job!"

I was quite offended. I wasn't sure what to do. The year before I had won a writing prize presented by a man named Judge Sweet. "If I can ever help you," he said, "let me know." I decided I'd take him at his word. Judge Sweet was part-owner of the *Brantford Expositor*, so I figured he could help me out.

When I actually showed up at his office, Judge Sweet was aghast. He couldn't believe a sixteen-year-old was asking for work. Nevertheless, he phoned the other co-owner, W.B. Preston, and said, "This woman seems to need a job. Can you give her one?"

It was 1941 and all the businesses were in a tight spot. The boys and men had all gone off to Europe and gotten killed. People like Mr. Preston had to choose between hiring women and having no employees at all. Mr. Preston asked if I'd like to be a proofreader. I said yes, assuming I'd figure out what that meant when I started.

I began at seven-thirty the next morning. Text would come off the linotype machines and I learned from the guy next to me, who actually knew what he was doing. At about nine or ten o'clock, the paper came out and they didn't need us anymore, so they made me an afternoon reporter. At first, they gave me the job nobody wanted, which involved going to the post office across the street and collecting the announcements from small communities in the area. I edited the information together, threw a headline on it, spiked it, and sent it upstairs to the linotypes. After that, I hit the streets on assignment. I worked from seven-thirty in the morning to ten-thirty at night and earned $7.50 a week. I gave half to my mother and lived off $3.75. It was fantastic.

Moving to Toronto

The feminist movement had started, but I was the last to get on board. I couldn't understand what everyone was crying about. I thought being a woman was a huge advantage. I didn't want to start working. I wanted to get married and have babies. The problem was that I was only seventeen and every time I started dating someone, they went overseas and got killed.

One day, the *Toronto Star* saw my byline in the *Expositor* and told me if I came to the city they'd give me $25 a week. They needed women writers and they thought my stuff was pretty good. I jumped at the chance and was out the door in seconds.

When I arrived, I looked about twelve years old. I hadn't physically developed as a woman yet. The management were aghast at what they'd done, hiring someone without asking their age. So they made me a secretary. Within two weeks, the editors could see I couldn't do it and fired me.

I went to the *Toronto Telegram* and applied there. But their editorial staff had the same reaction and offered me a secretary position. I knew I couldn't keep doing that, so I went off to join the Air Force. I told them I wanted to fly fighter planes and they told me I could be a secretary too.

I went back to the only newspaper left: *The Globe and Mail*. I arrived at the office around lunch hour. There didn't seem to be anyone around. The managing editor's secretary was on break, so I walked casually into his office and stood in front of him. Eventually, he peered up and said, "You look like you want a job." I told him my story — or at least some of it — and he said, "If you'll cover the Ontario Medical Association Convention at the Royal York Hotel and write about it for the Monday paper, I'll see what I can do."

Down I went with my little notepad. The conference consisted of simultaneous workshop meetings. I couldn't make head nor tail of any of it and I couldn't follow any of the speeches. It was horrible. Luckily, I met a reporter from the *Toronto Star*. "I don't know how to write this," I said to him. "And I'm on probation from the *Globe*." He said he could write the article for me. He wrote one for himself and another for me. The *Globe* hired me on the basis of another reporter's work. With perks like that, why would I want to be a feminist?

Marriage

Male reporters were always eager to help me out. I eventually married one of them. Trent Frayne was a sportswriter at the *Globe*. He was a very good journalist and I knew almost instantly that I wanted to marry him. He was twenty-six and I was nineteen when we finally tied the knot. The newspaper didn't allow married women on staff, so when we announced our engagement, they were petrified. They desperately wanted to keep me. The *Globe* told me that I had to keep my maiden name, so that readers wouldn't know I was married. That's why I'm still June Callwood today! It had nothing to do with being a feminist.

I assumed that, as soon as I had babies, I'd quit and become a stay-at-home mom. I always thought ten little ones would be about right.

As soon as I looked pregnant, the *Globe* refused to keep me on staff any longer. At the time, that was fine with me. But after my child was born, they hired me back on a temporary basis. They asked me to cover fashion shows, of all things!

Pilot June

Gradually, I came to realize that raising a baby didn't take up all of my time. I decided I wanted to learn how to fly. Most of the men I had dated in Brantford had been pilots and I covered the Brantford Air Force base at the *Expositor*. Flying had an undeniable romantic magnetism for me.

I went to Barker Field, just north of Eglinton Avenue in Toronto. My instructor was a woman named Vi Milstead. At twenty-four, she joined the British Air Transport Auxiliary and flew new Spitfires from factories to military bases across England and Allied Europe. She was a fantastically inspiring woman and I desperately wanted to write a story on her. The problem was that I knew I couldn't sell it to the *Globe*. Newspapers didn't do personality stories back then. So I approached *Liberty Magazine* and they bought it for $50. That's what got me started as a freelancer.

Freelancing

In its Canadian incarnation, *Liberty Magazine* was edited by a man named Jim Harris. Back in the 1940s, a lot of writers got started there, mainly because Jim didn't know what he was doing. He didn't have any standards, and as a result, people like me became magazine writers without ever knowing how to do so.

Toronto had a number of magazines that would buy articles. There was *Saturday Night*, *Home and Garden*, *Chatelaine*, and *Maclean's*, the prestige one. In the mid-1940s, *Maclean's* was edited by W. Arthur Irwin. He hired me to write about fashion because he had seen the pieces I had done for the *Globe*. I had been warned that Irwin was notoriously slow at getting back to writers. "His trick is to be absolutely silent on the phone," I was told by one reporter. "You say something and he won't answer, so you babble on and on. That's his trick."

After I submitted the fashion piece Irwin wanted, I waited six weeks without hearing a response. When he finally phoned me to say he wasn't going to buy it, I spoke up. "You'll have to pay me," I said. "It was a perishable piece and it's too late for me to sell it to anyone else. I have to be paid in full." There was complete silence on the other end of the line, just as I had been warned. I had a chocolate bar in a little desk drawer next to the phone, so I pulled it out and slowly ate the entire thing over the phone. In the end, he cracked and agreed to pay me in full. I had out-waited him. Afterwards, I received much faster service.

Making the transition from newspaper stories to the 3,000- to 5,000-word pieces that *Maclean's* ran wasn't too difficult. As long as you can find a story's spine, it's relatively easy to tell it in as many words as necessary. Story length isn't as important as people outside the business think. A book is far easier to write than a short story. Books offer you all sorts of elbow room.

Maclean's

Maclean's real glory years started in 1950, when Ralph Allen became editor. He was a marvellous writer and teacher. I wrote on everything you could imagine in those days: Marilyn Bell's swim across Lake Ontario, Oscar Peterson, Rocket Richard, and the Avro Arrow — can you imagine giving that one to a woman? I did a series on life in the St. Michael's Hospital emergency ward and another on life inside a convent.

I'd pound out a story, drive it down to the office, and deliver it to Ralph. Back then, we all had only one copy. Journalists got tired of keeping a carbon and then disposing of it and writing things again. After I'd drop my story off, I'd wait by the phone for Ralph's call. He was renowned for the comments he'd make in the margins. My husband still recalls finding "Give this man a box of Snickers" next to a section Ralph felt was overwritten. Another time, it said, "This reads like the withered leaves of Elmer Ferguson's diary." Thankfully, I hardly ever got comments. Invariably, the phone would ring and Ralph would say, "Callwood's done it again!" I'd give anything to hear that again.

The *Maclean's* team was a real gang back then. We'd have dinners at each other's houses every Friday. We'd have a casserole, a salad, a case of beer, and a bottle of rye. Nobody left until all the booze was gone. It was a wonderful time.

Advocacy Journalism

It's tough for young people to imagine, but there used to be a lot of public pressure to write happy and supportive stories. I remember doing a magazine piece on the Happy Gang, a team of CBC radio DJs. The story revealed that, in reality, the Happy Gang hated one another. I got a lot of hostile mail after that story ran.

The first time I realized my duty to present more than an airbrushed version of reality was when I was writing about a young virtuoso pianist named Patsy Carr. She was eleven or twelve years old and I could see how her mother dominated her and how unhappy she was. Instead of writing about how amazing this young girl was, I wrote the truth: that she was a miserable child prodigy. That was very much ahead of its time in Canada. Back in the 1950s, no one was doing much honesty. From that point on, I was a much better reporter.

Gradually, my work focused more on the ails of society and the people who were being ignored or tossed aside. As a journalist, you can only do so much. There is a Chinese wall between journalism and social activism. The journalist cannot cross it. You can't write about the people you're trying to help. You can't write about the things you're doing on the other side of the wall. What you can do, however, is take off your journalism hat and make a difference. It's a tricky line to walk, but it's important.

In the 1970s and 1980s, I was writing a social criticism column for the *Globe* and working shifts in a women's hostel. Some of the stories of the women who came through the door were so poignant, they were a journalist's dream. But while working there, I never wrote about any of it.

Today

I couldn't imagine getting started in journalism today. A person like me wouldn't have a chance in journalism school. Besides, I'm not sure they're good places to learn journalism. They're technical — they can't teach you how to learn or feel. All they teach is the stuff everyone knows anyway: how to write a lead and how to write a paragraph. You need a heck of a lot more than that to be a writer.

DIANE DUPUY

*"Everything happens for a reason, and sometimes we have
to be prepared for the unexpected in order to learn from it."*

In the west end of Toronto, between a pastry factory and a used car lot, there's an old converted warehouse that houses the Famous PEOPLE Players. The troupe residing there, formed by **Diane Dupuy** at the age of twenty-six, is made up of mentally disabled performers who put on black light spectacles six times a week, all year round. The company has, since its creation in 1976, toured the world, including long stretches on Broadway and in Las Vegas. They have amassed celebrity endorsements across the board, from Liberace and Paul Newman to Pierre Trudeau — many of whom became close friends with Dupuy.

The same imagination that inspired the Famous PEOPLE Players has also gotten Dupuy through difficult personal situations. Her childhood recollections show what she was up against: an alcoholic father, an early life spent picking raspberries for three dollars a day, being teased by her classmates, failing Grade 3, failing Grade 6, failing Grade 9 twice. Escape for Dupuy has always been something that existed despite — and in many ways was reinforced by — the turmoil in her life.

Playing with Nature

I lived in the woods. Our backyard went out into Ontario's Niagara Escarpment, and since my brother and I didn't have toys or computer games, we had to play with nature. We were out in the woods from early morning until suppertime. It was fabulous. We had the freedom to go wherever we wanted. There was a favourite tree that we would climb. We used to sit up there; he would be Robin Hood, I would be the Lone Ranger. When autumn came, we gathered the fallen leaves, swept them together, and made a house with a living room, a dining room, and a kitchen.

When the municipality decided to put a highway through the area, we sold our house, said goodbye, and moved to Hamilton. My mother opened a fashion store and we lived upstairs. Even though I missed the woods, I found other ways to escape. My mother would hang our laundry out — underwear and all, for the neighbors to see — and after collecting it in a basket to bring back into the house, we'd always keep one sheet out. Pretending it was a curtain, I would put on puppet shows for the neighbourhood kids. My brother and I would then make lemonade, set up a little stand, and sell it to whoever came by.

I never did well in school for two reasons: I was living with an alcoholic father, which was very dramatic, and I was picked on by the other students. I would blank out and imagine I was riding an invisible horse. I turned off the real world, never paying much attention to the things around me. School never challenged me; it was extremely boring. I failed so many grades because I just didn't care. I didn't want to try. Even though I only have a Grade 8 education, believe me, I learned to hustle in other ways. I had to work. We had to turn lemons into lemonade.

When I was twenty-seven, I quit playing professional football. I'd been traded from Ottawa to Toronto the year before. I left the team because I had insisted during away games that they fly me back to attend Sunday church services. They said it wasn't going to work out.

Later that year, I found my calling. As a registered minister, I travelled around preaching to different churches throughout Ontario. One Sunday, I gave a sermon at the Evangelical Church of the Deaf in Toronto. While I spoke from the pulpit, the eyes of the congregation weren't on me: they were watching the sign language interpreter below. I spoke simply and clearly to them, and when I finished, they wanted to know if I could hang around because they needed a full-time minister. I saw they needed my help. Even though I knew nothing about sign language, I agreed — but these deaf people didn't know what they were getting into.

— **Bob Rumball**, former CFL halfback and founder of the Bob Rumball Centre for the Deaf

Youth Opportunities

From the age of sixteen to twenty-two, I worked as a sales clerk in a bunch of stores — probably every clothing store across Hamilton. I thought I was enjoying it because it brought in a paycheque and I didn't know what to do with my life. But I was only at a crossroads, just passing time. Everything happens for a reason, and sometimes we have to be prepared for the unexpected in order to learn from it. Until then, life may be discouraging or hurtful, but the answer will be waiting down the road.

When I was about twenty-two, Prime Minister Pierre Trudeau introduced job creation. The government would offer grants to anyone who had a unique idea for a job or a project of some sort. So I came up with the idea of black light puppet shows and called it the Famous PEOPLE Players.

In my spare time, I started putting on shows. It was basically the same thing I had been doing as a kid, only this time I was getting paid for it — though not very much. I had a little stage and I'd carry it around to malls and schools, performing with hand puppets. I even had a Trudeau puppet that waltzed around with Barbara Streisand, a comical reference to the supposed affair between the two.

At one point, I was asked to come and put on a show at the Surrey Place Centre in Toronto. It was for people who were labelled "mentally retarded" — that was the terminology used back then. I didn't want to do it because I didn't know anything about these kinds of people, but I ended up getting talked into it.

The response was electric. The kids were rapt with attention. I'd never seen that kind of focus, that kind of amazement. At one point, a little girl started to have a seizure and the others gathered around and helped her up until the supervisor came over. I saw the care and interest these kids had.

Unfortunately, they weren't given a chance to be creative in the outside world. I decided to try and integrate them into society. What I did was completely unheard of. At that time, the kids ended up at this big institution in Orillia where they had sheltered workshops. They were taught simple trades: how to work on an assembly line and things like that. A school bus would pick them up and take them to a school for the "mentally retarded." I asked myself, What kind of a life is that?

The schools didn't want the kids to be involved in a theatre group because to them it would be a freak show. I was only asking for a few students who I would be able to direct and, at the very last minute, I was given ten people, with no choice on who they were. Believe me, they were the worst ten. They couldn't follow orders, didn't understand anything, and were seriously disabled. You couldn't get anything done with them. On the first day, I realized that what I thought would be running a theatre company turned out to be a whole life-skills program.

The Troupe

I managed to get us some gigs at a mall. We worked on one routine to start. It involved a fluorescent piano, lots of instruments, and life-size puppets all dancing around to music. During our first public performance, the piano rolled off the stage and into the audience. The second show wasn't much better: the piano rolled right across the stage and off the other side. We were bad.

It only started to improve day by day. I never took my eye off the finishing line. I was a horse with blinders on and we kept rehearsing and we kept dancing and we kept ironing out the routines. Once we got our first number down, I was proud of the performers. The song was called "Aruba Liberace," which included a huge puppet of Liberace in a white tuxedo.

We put so much work into it that I wanted to tell the singer himself. I wrote countless letters to Las Vegas but never heard back. I tried calling, too, but couldn't get through because I was a nobody; I was only Diane Dupuy. I wanted to talk to his manager, but every day they gave the same response. The secretary would ask for my name and, when I told her, would say he was in a conference or out for lunch, and to call back later. It was frustrating.

Something had to be done. If Liberace noticed us, the Famous PEOPLE Players would get their foot in the door and everyone would notice the great things we were doing. I needed a new approach, so I got creative. I phoned again, this time pretending to be Prime Minister Trudeau's secretary. I told them Mr. Trudeau had seen this giant puppet of Liberace and wanted to know if he could book a spot for the Emperor of Japan's upcoming visit. They didn't know what to say.

The next day, I called up as myself. When they found out that *I* was the girl who had the routine for "Aruba Liberace," life-size figure and all, I was finally put through to Liberace's manager. When we spoke, he seemed very interested. Within a few months, we arranged a time for Liberace to come and see the show for himself in Toronto.

Even though technically it was founded on a lie, I didn't see it as such because I was in a position where I had nothing to lose. At the time, it just seemed like a creative way to reach a specific end. We needed that notoriety from Liberace — which helped us get our first show in Las Vegas as his opening act, which led to Broadway and eventually a world tour — and had I not lied, we would never have had that success.

I have these inspirational moments where out of nowhere I get an idea and I go with it. So when I'm asked, "How did it happen?" Well, I don't know — it just happened. And that sort of thing happens because I have a mind grown out of nature, one that rarely reflects and never makes plans. I learned to climb to the top of trees without thinking.

EDWARD BURTYNSKY

"Being told I couldn't shoot in colour just made me want to do it more. I felt I could be a pioneer."

Edward Burtynsky is one of the world's most acclaimed and relevant living photographers. His large-format and richly textured images of industrial landscapes have forced the public to acknowledge the sublime, but deeply disturbing, effect of accelerated industrialization. An inaugural winner of the TED Prize for innovation and global thinking, Burtynsky's work was the inspiration for Jennifer Baichwal's documentary *Manufactured Landscapes*, which was named Best Canadian Film at the 2006 Toronto International Film Festival and was nominated for the Grand Jury Prize at the 2007 Sundance Film Festival.

At eleven, Burtynsky received his first camera. When his first two rolls of Tri-X film ran out, his father told him that if he wanted to take more pictures, he'd have to support the habit on his own. Burtynsky began photographing events at his local Ukrainian Community Centre and charging fifty cents a shot. "The experience taught me that simple entrepreneurial solutions can exist if you really have a will to do something," the soft-spoken photographer recalls. The money he made at the community centre supported his habit, allowing him to wander through the countryside near his native St. Catharines, Ontario, capturing images of landscapes and abandoned warehouses. While he loved the challenges of compressing the world into two dimensions, Burtynsky didn't think of photography as a sensible career. He thought he would need to be a commercial artist instead.

Is There a Future in This?

The more I played with my camera, the more I knew I wanted to be an art photographer. I didn't want to be a portrait photographer or a wedding photographer. I didn't want to be a reporter or a social photographer either. I didn't want to be a gun for hire. I wanted to use photography the way a painter used oil paints or watercolours. I wanted to use photography to explore and learn about the world.

Growing up in my environment, that kind of life didn't feel like a real option. St. Catharines is a brawny, blue-collar town. There isn't a high level of sensitivity towards the development of creative skills. Looking around, I couldn't see any way to make a living doing what I wanted to do. As a result, I decided to make the practical choice and enrol in the graphic arts program at Niagara College. I could do printing, prepress, layout, design, and drawing. Photography and plate-making were involved as well. I figured it was the closest thing to art photography that might give me a real future.

Finding a Subject in Your Backyard

Growing up in St. Catharines, you can't help but be affected by and interested in industrial sites. They are part of your day-to-day experience. I was fascinated with them.

As a kid, factories were mysterious places. People seemed wholly disconnected from them. The world experienced their products on a daily basis, but few people had any idea what went on inside. I used to walk past the forge plant near our home, hear the *Bam! Bam! Bam!* emanating from inside, and try to imagine what was going on behind the walls. When I finally got to see for myself, the scene of red-hot ingots being poured out and all these men in aluminum suits was surreal. It wasn't at all like I'd imagined.

Since that's where the money was, those industrial environments were eventually where I worked to pay my way through school. At seventeen, I worked at Hayes-Dana, a large plant that built truck frames for GM. Later, I worked at the GM and Ford plants as well. I did two years on production lines. That was as much of a taste as I wanted. The problem was that the pay made it very seductive. Guys would start out with no intention of staying, but then they would get a huge mortgage on their house, buy a big car, and suddenly their lives would be sucked into the vortex of factory life, never to emerge again. Working there made me focus on getting out of that world.

Though hungry for escape, I was also hungry to learn as much as I could. "What's going on here?" I'd ask myself. "How does it all work?" If they wanted someone to work on a particular line, I'd always be the first to volunteer. Then I'd figure it out and be able to do something new. I've always felt that, whatever you're doing, you should put your best foot forward. I don't care if you're flipping hamburgers. Try to learn as much as you can and try to engage with the people around you. If you tell people that you want to do something, they'll eventually let you do it. You can't be bashful. You have to ask. If they don't know you're interested, they're not going to go out of their way to make it happen.

Those years of working on production lines and learning about industrial processes informed my view of the world and the type of work I would eventually do.

You Can't Escape Your Talent

While I worked at the factories and completed my courses, I never stopped shooting. Living in Canada, we're blessed to have an enormous amount of raw nature at our fingertips. I was in awe of the unspoilt and I tried to capture as much of it with my camera as possible. Eventually, I began taking night classes in pure photography. That's when I realized I couldn't escape it: photography was what I needed to be doing. My teacher recognized a natural affinity and suggested I go to Ryerson in Toronto.

By that point, I was almost finished two years of college. The idea of four more years at Ryerson seemed ridiculous. But when I came down to

Edward Burtynsky: "If you tell people that you want to do something, they'll eventually let you do it."

the city and toured the campus, my attitude changed. Suddenly, I realized that I had the opportunity to be doing what I always wanted to be doing. The idea of being an art photographer didn't feel strange or impossible anymore. A whole world was opening up. All I had to do was take a chance.

And I got in. The four-year program laid out the history of art, the history of photography, music, psychology, and philosophy — everything you needed to start thinking about your art.

Finding New Forms

The faculty members at Ryerson were amazing. They'd always push me to try new things. I'd give something a shot and then move on, realizing it wasn't what I wanted to do. I tried street photography for six months with a 35-mm Leica, for example. I got some great shots, but it didn't get my juices flowing. I realized that my heart was in landscapes — going out with large-format cameras and methodically creating images. I wanted to "make" images rather than simply "take" them. Street photography was all about responding to your environment, snapping a lot of shots, and then picking the best ones. With larger formats, you approach your subject in a more contemplative way.

In my second year, we were exposed to colour labs. It was as though someone had flicked a switch in my head. I loved it and started shooting colour negatives immediately. At the time, teachers would tell you that colour was commercial and brash. Apparently, art photography had to be in black and white. I didn't buy it. Being told I couldn't shoot in colour just made me want to do it more. I felt I could be a pioneer. Looking back, the whole argument between colour and black and white seems laughable now.

Getting Experience and Dealing with Debt

After the third year, I took some time off. I was broke and deeply in debt. I've always hated the idea of being in that position, so I took a couple of years and worked in the corporate sector. First, I got a job in IBM's photography department, doing plates for government cheques in Ottawa. After about a year, I was hired by the Ontario Hospital Association. The OHA distributes information about new legislation and developments to its member hospitals. They sent me to hospitals with writers to shoot the photos for the stories they'd be covering in their newsletters.

The best thing about the OHA job was that I had the opportunity to start a photography department from scratch. I was given a large empty space and it was up to me to build a darkroom and a studio and buy all the equipment. I had a $250,000 budget and I was able to source out all the equipment. Suddenly, I was making connections in the industry. It took me a year and a half to build the department, but that experience was a training ground for starting my own photo lab down the line.

Surviving the Transition

After those years off, I was able to put myself through the last year at Ryerson with enough savings to continue paying off my debts while I was in school. I graduated in 1982, and within three weeks of the ceremony, I got my first Canada Council grant. I went to Ottawa, applied, and four weeks later I had the money. That made the post-university transition so much easier. It's a tender moment when you first come out of school. You've got debts and you don't have a job. You're pretty insecure. But to say "I've got a Canada Council grant" — that meant people thought what I was doing was worthwhile. It made the transition much easier.

The subject of my project was "industrial greenhouses": these artificial worlds we'd started creating to extend growing seasons. I visited seventy to eighty greenhouses throughout Southern Ontario. I initially honed in on a few and then started asking people if they could refer me to people with equally interesting structures. I wanted to explore how these constructions, which sought to recreate natural landscapes, could be seen as landscapes in and of themselves.

The grant money wasn't perfect, but it was enough. Gradually, I started selling my work. There wasn't a huge commercial market for the stuff I was doing, but a lot of institutions in Ottawa were buying. The Canada Council Art Bank was purchasing work and the National Film Board Stills Division (which is now the Canadian Museum of Contemporary Photography) was buying some as well.

Finding Ways to Survive

To stay afloat, I needed to do freelance work in architectural photography. It was large format and the pace and process were similar to landscape photography, so I actually enjoyed and learned from it. In fact, I still do quite a bit of architectural photography. It keeps my vision honed and suits my temperament.

In 1985, I started the Toronto Image Works lab. I had a peppered job history and no real lab experience, but I wanted to start a business and felt there was a market for it. I went to all the places I was trying to emulate and I took note of what they were doing right and what they were doing wrong. The biggest mistake I saw was that they were all rather hodgepodge operations. A guy would save up $50,000, build four darkrooms, buy four enlargers and a twenty-four-inch processor and a counter, and then buy and build more down the line. As far as I saw it, you could never keep a loyal client base that way. I went out and bough the best of everything: the best enlargers, the best lenses, the best darkrooms. I also created a dark area so people wouldn't have to repackage their paper. You lose so much from kinks and dents. We had a microswitch so all the power would go off in the darkroom and in the hallway. That way, you could feed in the print right away without having to repackage your paper to keep it lightsafe.

Because I put in all this thinking, when I went to banks and investors, I could honestly tell them I had the ultimate solution. I could confidently say that with 1.5 million people in Toronto and a university that needed a place for their overflow to go when their darkrooms got too busy, there was a definite market. I was asking for $250,000 and people responded because they respected how methodical my approach had been. Those same darkrooms and lenses I bought then are still here twenty years later.

The Freedom to Play

Running Toronto Image Works vastly improved the technical side of my work. I suddenly gained an intimate understanding of the difference between films, papers, and materials. Painters are always interested in why someone would use oil versus acrylic paint or how someone would dress their canvas. I didn't think there was any reason why photographers shouldn't ask similar questions. Running Toronto Image Works also gave me the chance to experience new products just as they were coming on the market. Having the lab put me in a similar position to the one I was in as an eleven-year-old kid: I wasn't worried about how much things cost or whether I was wasting material. Suddenly, I was playing again.

In 1987, when I put on a show at the Canadian Museum of Contemporary Photography, I fought with them about print size. I wanted to do thirty-by-forty prints. They considered that just outrageous. They insisted on twenty-by-twenty-four. To them, that was the largest any print could ever be. After that, I started doing bigger prints on my own at my lab and went out in search of galleries to take my work. In New York, I found two — Larry Miller and Lieberman & Saul — and had to choose between them. Soon after, I had a dealer in New York, and then, in 1992, I had one in Toronto as well.

Now, I'm able to do the type of work I want to do.

"Despite all of our success, we always lived in fear of the financial squeeze."

As the founder of Barrick Gold, the world's largest gold mining company, **Peter Munk** is one of the highest rollers in Canadian business. A generous philanthropist, he has established a charitable foundation, made whopping donations to the Toronto General Hospital, and funded the esteemed Munk Centre for International Studies at the University of Toronto. Things weren't always so good, though. The Nazi invasion of Hungary forced his aristocratic Jewish family to flee Budapest for Zurich, Switzerland. Later, he moved to Toronto as a student.

As war raged throughout Europe, Munk never guessed that, ten years later, he would be the face of a new entrepreneurial spirit in Canada, a country he'd hardly heard of at the time. But that's what happened. During the 1960s, Clairtone, the high-end electronics company he founded with his partner, David Gilmour, was the freshest and most exciting player on the Canadian business scene. Thanks to groundbreaking brand management and the company's revolutionary "Project G" series stereo, Clairtone grew at breakneck speed and became synonymous with the youthful style of the age. Its ultimate collapse in 1970 is still a sore spot for the man many people once considered a potential prime minister, but Munk's story bears lessons for anyone looking to make their mark.

A Transportable Skill

There was never any question of studying anything but engineering. It was the late 1940s and the world was in turmoil. My family didn't know if we would end up as agricultural labourers in Palestine or as part of the Communist empire, so I needed a transportable skill — something that would get me work wherever I ended up. Everyone always needed engineers.

The war had destroyed the majority of the great universities in Europe.

Once peace was declared, people flooded into neutral Switzerland to attend its schools. This made it especially difficult for me to get into a Swiss engineering program. After three years of trying and failing, my parents decided I should attend school in Canada and live with my uncle Nick, a Toronto resident since the 1930s. When they told me, I cried. I had never really heard of Canada. It was too far away from Europe.

Arriving in Canada

When my uncle Nick picked me up at Union Station, the first thing he told me was, "We don't speak any language here but English." It didn't matter that I hardly knew a word of English.

Before I left Switzerland, my father gave me $350 for my tuition. Just before university began, I went to New York and blew every penny. While I was there, I met a girl. She was stunningly beautiful and we went to the El Morocco nightclub where all the stars hung out. There didn't seem to be any option but to spend like mad.

After coming back with nothing, I asked Uncle Nick for a loan, but he refused, saying he wasn't a bank and that I was responsible for my actions. I explained the situation to my barber while I was having a trim and he told me that I could make $10 a day plus room and board as a tobacco picker in late August. So, for forty-one days, just outside of Guelph, I woke up at 5:00 a.m. to pick tobacco until nightfall. I came back sick and miserable, but with enough cash in my pocket to handle my tuition.

A Mere Distraction

As far as I was concerned, my studies at the University of Toronto were unimportant. I just wanted to have a good time: to go to football games, go out on dates, and party as much as possible. Finding a job that could support my extracurricular interests seemed much more important than going to my electrical engineering classes. During my undergraduate years, I worked at a carwash and at a post office sorting letters — the types of jobs where I could earn good money but still stay focused on school.

By the time I reached my third year, I was an entrepreneur. Two weeks before Christmas, I asked my uncle if I could use his front lawn. "For what?" he asked. I told him I wanted to put up a little stand. He lived in a high-traffic area and I reckoned I could sell Christmas trees in front of the house. "You'll freeze," he said. I didn't care. I went and bought pine trees wholesale, paying seventy-five cents to a dollar each and then sold them for three to four bucks a pop from his lawn. It was a phenomenal business model.

The next year, I got a few of my fellow students together and phoned the local grocery stores, asking if we could use their parking lots. "We're not going to let you kids sell Christmas trees here," they said. I knew my plan would work. "Your customers come here, park, and buy dinner for Christmas," I said. "Why should the poor suckers have to go and park somewhere else to get a tree?" Finally, two or three stores agreed and I paid them a hundred bucks each.

The business grew and grew. We set up an office in downtown Toronto, incorporated the company (calling ourselves Student Co-Op Sales), and borrowed several thousand dollars in the summertime to buy trees at the lowest possible price. By the third year, I had school kids minding lots all over the city and I was making 20 percent of all the profits.

That year, just before Christmas, the city was hit by the biggest snowstorm in a decade. It lasted three days. All our trees were stuck in the lots because the kids couldn't make it to work. Christmas passed by and we barely sold anything. Afterwards, we couldn't give the trees away. We just left them in the lots. Though I almost went bankrupt, I learned a valuable lesson: there's no fail-safe way to invest money. Logic and sound planning can all be annulled by the good lord. You have to cover your ass. It wasn't a great philosophical lesson, but it was a good one for business.

The Working World

After school finished, I took a job at CN Telegraph. They put me in charge of designing telegraph lines. It was insanely tedious work because every telegraph line was the same. Canada's a big country: millions of power lines were needed, stretching to the horizon in all directions. I found it hard to stay awake. I survived the mornings, but every afternoon I would fall asleep. The money was good and my boss was nice, so I wanted to do a good job, but I couldn't. I knew I would eventually have to leave.

Luckily, my uncle found me a job with Atlas Radio. They were the first players in Canada to start importing high-fidelity components. Hi-fis were becoming a huge craze at the time — much like personal computers twenty-five years later. I figured that once I was in the loop, I could buy the stereos wholesale, assemble the equipment myself, and sell units to my friends and their parents. Because I wasn't a retailer with high overhead costs, I was free to sell the systems at low prices and still make money. Atlas Radio didn't mind, and since I was a good customer it ended up being a great deal for both of us.

Peter Munk & Associates

After selling hi-fis to friends for a while, I began importing used television sets from the United States. At the time, the Americans were throwing away units that were newer and more advanced than the ones being sold on the Canadian market. The American retailers ran huge ads that said, "Turn in your old TV set and get a new one!" I approached the retailers, asking to buy the hand-ins. For $30 to $40, I got televisions that were being sold for $250 in Canada. When I came back, I hired a part-time TV repairman from Atlas and a woodworker to help make the sets look newer. Then I put little ads in the newspaper saying "Used TV sets for half price." The demand was incredible.

Eventually, I was served with a legal letter claiming I was infringing on Canadian patents. The big television manufacturers were protecting the Canadian market by ensuring that all retailers had to buy from them. I didn't even know what a patent was, but my lawyer told me to desist because it could pose serious problems.

By that time, I had sold hundreds of sets and I had a little workshop full of woodworkers. When I had to stop selling televisions, I switched back to hi-fi machines and started putting them in nice cabinets.

One day, my father-in-law sat me down and suggested that I start my own business. He could see that I was selling a lot of hi-fis through Atlas and thought I could make more money working for myself. "That's easy for you to say," I replied. "It's hard for me to take chances. I'm married to your daughter!"

"That's precisely why you should," he said. "Except you'll need to do it full-time. Don't wait for anyone to come to you. Go and find customers while you're still at Atlas. Then when you leave, you'll have a secure base." He asked me to figure out how much capital I would need, and ended up giving me $2,800, on the condition that my family would match the figure. With around $5,000, I started Peter Munk & Associates and set up an office in Toronto, determined to take my custom-built hi-fi stereo units onto the market.

The Soviet Union

Growing up, I had always been very left wing. My mother had been sent to Auschwitz, and seeing the Communists fight the Nazis and liberate the camps had a large effect on me. Don't ask how I reconciled my left-wing leanings with my desire to make money: I wasn't the deepest thinker.

In 1958, an exchange program with the Soviet Union was set up by the

National Federation of Canadian University Students. My wife, a second-year student at Victoria College at the time, found the ad and showed it to me. I told her I'd give my life to go, so we raised $2,000 (a large sum at the time) and became part of the eighteen-student delegation.

During the trip, I realized everything our tour guides said, everything the Soviet Union was telling the world about itself, was a lie. In Kiev, some of the Ukrainian Canadians among our delegation pretended not to speak Ukrainian and snuck off during the tour, returning with stories of beatings and mass starvation. Gradually, we began to sneak away more and more, trying to get something other than the "official truth."

I was so angry that I seriously considered giving up my fledgling business career to go from campus to campus, educating Canadian students about the lies of Communism. My politics changed completely after that trip.

The Beginning of Something

My future business partner, David Gilmour, was a central figure in the social scene I ran with. He came from one of the country's oldest and most connected families, and his sister ran the hippest and most successful furniture business on Toronto's Bloor Street. She sold sleek and modern Scandinavian designs before anyone else caught on to the trend. David worked as a buyer for her before starting a business called Scantrade, which imported Swedish and Norwegian furniture to stores across the city.

Peter Munk with his former business partner David Gilmour: "The press loved that David and I recognized our different and complementary skill sets."

As it became increasingly clear that people wanted hi-fi stereos stored in fashionable, modern furniture units, David approached me about handling the components that would go in his cabinets. After I had provided him with a few installations, we starting talking about a more ambitious endeavour. "I can get these cabinets wholesale," he said. "Do you think it's worthwhile to buy ten and standardize a product?" I went around to see what Simpson's and Eaton's and the other big retailers were selling. I was astounded. They got $400 a pop for poor-quality merchandise. I knew that with his designs and my engineering, we could do much better. At our company, we'd sold around five hundred machines in two years. I knew people would pay for quality and David's success proved that people loved beautiful, high-end designs. We stood to make a huge margin.

We never aimed to start a bike company. We wanted to sell our prototype to one of the big European companies, but they didn't bite. Our design was too expensive for them to build. We were confident that if we constructed our own tubes, stays, and forks, and put the models together ourselves, we'd produce the most aerodynamic bike on the market. With the support of other cyclists, we decided to start Cervélo.

After pooling together our resources and seeking out investment from friends, we had about $50,000. We started running the company out of a student room in Montreal, but after relocating to Toronto, we made an office out of the spare bedroom in Phil and his wife's house. We lived on $50 a week. Every dime we ever made went right back into the company. We couldn't even pay ourselves for the first five years. Luckily, we didn't have extravagant needs. Throughout those early years, we knew the bikes would blow people away. We wouldn't have put ourselves through it if we didn't know we'd be successful in the end.

— **Phil White and Gérard Vroomen**, founders of Cervélo Cycles, the only North American manufacturer to supply top Tour de France riders

The Birth of Clairtone

David and I spent six months at the end of 1957 perfecting our models. Then, when we were sure we had a great product, we incorporated Clairtone. The company consisted of the core staff from Peter Munk & Associates, plus David. I was president and David was a vice-president. At the beginning, we offered two standard models: a monaural high-fidelity unit and a stereophonic unit, both housed in low-slung Scandinavian cabinets with sliding doors. We charged $599 for the hi-fi and $695 for the stereo design, knowing that we could target people who wanted quality and had the money to pay for it.

After showcasing the models to the major distributors, orders began flooding in. By November of the next year, we had to move into a five-thousand-square-foot factory space. We were too busy to even think about our finances. We started the company with $3,500 in capital, and after a seven-month period, we had made a net profit of $28,555, before taxes.

The problem was that every cent coming in the door went toward buying new components. Not only did we go without earning any salary, but we were heavily overdrawn, with many outstanding cheques. Luckily, the numbers were good enough to impress our banker and secure an extended loan.

Keeping the Dream Alive

Clairtone's success was a whirlwind. We were winning design awards and getting all kinds of positive attention. The press loved that David and I had recognized our different and complementary skill sets. They loved our enthusiasm too. Almost right off the bat, we began gunning for the American market and soon we were succeeding there as well.

Despite all of our success, we always lived in fear of the financial squeeze. David ultimately took out a mortgage on his house to free up cash when we needed it. He didn't ask for a note or any security. He just handed me the cheque and walked out.

We continually survived by the skin of our teeth. Even with David's family connections in the investment community, no one was in a hurry to back a pair of upstarts in a heavily competitive field. In 1961, when we bought up a smaller company from Strathroy, Ontario, to guarantee our supply of cabinets, our underwriters were about to back out. Luckily, I was given the number of J.H. Beatty, the governor of the Bank of Canada. I phoned him personally and explained what was at stake. All he said was, "Thank you for telling me, Mr. Munk. Goodbye." I thought I'd failed, but the next day, our underwriters said they could find a way to get us the money. That's how it goes when you're starting your own business. You have to put everything on the line and push forward as hard and as intelligently as possible.

In the end, Clairtone fell apart. We had expanded too fast and stupidly launched into colour TVs just as the market was becoming oversupplied with Japanese sets. But it was an incredible ride.

"There's a part of me that would like to be an artist."

James Gosling still considers himself an Alberta boy. Though he hasn't resided in Canada for almost thirty years, he still finds the experience of living in the United States "a little weird." As the inventor of the Java universal programming language, one of the most practical and popular forms of software script in the world, he's done well for himself. Since completing Java in 1994, he has been elected to the United States National Academy of Engineering and has received the Order of Canada.

Suburban Calgary, where Gosling grew up, was not the most inspiring place for a computer engineer. The city's culture — in the early 1970s, as now — revolved around the oil business. As an escape, he would break into the computer lab at the University of Calgary to play computer games. His presence caught the attention of some members of the department, and instead of kicking him out, they hired him on as part of the faculty's support staff. Spending his free time with "a bunch of physicists" was a double benefit: he was let in to a strange new world and, luckily, had a passable excuse whenever he missed a high school class.

Being a Geek

Calgary was not a great place for a computer programmer like me. Industry number one was oil, then agriculture and tourism in some order. Doing high-tech stuff was definitely pretty weird. Being a geek made you an outcast.

I had first become interested in computers at the age of fourteen. After taking a guided tour of the University of Calgary's computer department, I noticed that the combination lock on the lab door was pretty simple. People would walk up and hit the four-button combination, making it very obvious which buttons they were touching. So I decided to sneak into the lab.

Because I spent all my free time experimenting on those computers, by the time I became an actual student at the university, I was very good at programming. My knowledge of the theory side, though, was lacking. That was the main thing I learned in the classroom.

For part-time jobs, I'd help out scientists and faculty members on projects they were working on. I even helped develop software that was used to take pictures of a satellite in space. At any one time, I would be working for several employers, which meant I was able to graduate from college with money in the bank. At my most insane, I think I had five part-time jobs.

Leaving Calgary

As part of my degree, I had taken a computer course centred around a very cool book on optimizing networks. It was written by some folks from Carnegie Mellon University in Pittsburgh. When I was contemplating postgraduate studies, that book kept popping into my mind, so I applied to the school's software institute. At the time, it was one of the largest computer departments in the United States. Unlike the other places where I applied, they actually accepted me.

As a doctoral student at Carnegie Mellon, I did all kinds of projects. It's a strange environment for a graduate student, since it's one of the most advanced research facilities in the world, and even though I was a low-level person doing slave labour at the beginning, I was working on cool projects with fascinating people. I absorbed a great deal simply from being around them. In that period, I was on the edge of a lot of development in networking. That became important for the Java programming later on.

Had I stayed in Calgary, the only job prospects were being a university professor, working at a bank, or working for an oil company. None of those appealed to me. I moved to Pittsburgh without knowing a soul — and I haven't lived in Canada since. I always consider myself Canadian, though. I'm not an American citizen. I still have my Canadian passport. Living in the United States is often a surreal experience, especially these days. It's a pretty hard thing to stomach. I think about it every now and then and it makes me twitch.

Staring Mindlessly at Stuff

It was in Pittsburgh that I became really interested in art galleries. The good thing about Carnegie Mellon was that the computer science department was down the block from a great gallery, the Carnegie Museum of Art. When I was working on really hard software projects, I found that wandering through an art gallery and staring mindlessly at stuff just made the problems flow better.

I've been a big art fan ever since. I've been to many museums. I'm torn in choosing my favourite. I guess it would have to be the Musée d'Orsay in Paris, followed pretty closely by the National Gallery in London and the Chicago Art Institute. These are all magnificent galleries. Currently, I live right in the middle of California and my house is literally fifteen minutes from San Francisco. I go there all the time to see the museums, especially the Legion of Honor and the Museum of Modern Art. San Francisco is a great place for culture.

There's a part of me that would like to be an artist. I do some stuff for Sun Microsystems. I did the design on the company T-shirts, but it was mostly just cartoons. It's just for fun. I have no illusions about having any actual talent.

One of the reasons for my success is that I've always been inquisitive. In medical school, I asked a lot of questions. I'd read books, but they didn't always have the answers, so I'd investigate through experiments and lab trials. Research is largely about asking the right questions.

Innovation today requires thorough knowledge. It's not something that simply comes naturally. Never again will we see someone with the wide-ranging human mind of Leonardo da Vinci. The amount of knowledge today is so extensive that one person couldn't encompass it all. To innovate in surgery, you have to know the field like nobody else. Creativity has become a function of the amount of knowledge in our minds rather than just a personal or genetic gift.

— **Tirone David**, Head of Cardiovascular Surgery at the Toronto General Hospital and President of the American Association for Thoracic Surgery

The Workforce

After graduating, I got my first job at IBM. That was thanks to a postgraduate arrangement where Carnegie Mellon had a joint project with them, half-staffed by the university and half-staffed by IBM. I initially became an official employee while I was still a student. When they hired me later, it wasn't much of a change.

In that industry, I realized that not everyone had become interested in computers at an early age. Computers are simple tools and can be useful when applied to something practical, so you have this interesting phenomenon where people dive into computer software after a completely different career. The combination with another background — like business or advertising — can be quite powerful.

While working at IBM, I knew a number of people at Sun

Microsystems. They would meet me undercover and ask me to join their company. The fact that I was working for such a massive organization helped their cause: Sun was much more flexible and innovative, with a certain affection for their employees. They had some enticing propositions and kept bugging me until, eventually, I couldn't say no anymore.

Moving to Sun was like coming to join a bunch of friends on a great adventure. It was a company that was open to weird and interesting ideas. Everyone had a lot of creativity. Working at smaller companies can be stressful at times, since they often have a day-to-day existence, but if you can live with that — if you have thick skin in dealing with a certain amount of stress — it can be very beneficial. I'm sure that, had I stayed at IBM, I would never have come up with something like Java.

Developing Java

We were working with different operating systems at Sun, investigating what was coming out and all the new programming. The technology wasn't necessarily changing, but its application was. It was becoming more embedded in society and new problems were arising. If you're dealing with society, you have to focus on connectivity: systems need to be in contact and share a common language.

No programming methodology existed. It was my job to go out and create it. The universal language was basically a way for systems to talk to each other. We needed a common infrastructure so we had to build systems that were secure and reliable. We had to adapt because the computer software world was always changing.

ROBERTA BONDAR

"The thing I learned, while moving from one domain to the next, was never to close doors behind me."

Roberta Bondar spent her childhood looking at the skies above Sault Ste. Marie, Ontario, searching for constellations and satellites. She was always a curious kid, poking her nose into anything of interest, which earned her the nickname "Ferret" among family members and teachers. The inquisitiveness continued well into her adult years, as she pursued degrees in zoology, agriculture, pathology, and neurobiology, finally getting an MD at the age of thirty-one.

In 1984, Bondar began astronaut training with the Canadian space program, and eight years later, as the space shuttle *Discovery* penetrated the atmosphere, she became the first Canadian woman in space. She has since become an internationally acclaimed author and photographer.

Studies

During my college years, I benefited from doing a little bit of everything. After a summer job at the local insectarium, I became fascinated by insects and decided to pursue an etymology course at the University of Guelph. Once there, I shifted my goal to becoming a high school science teacher and enrolled in a four-year honours degree in science. Since the university was recruiting students into a new agricultural program, literally paying us to join, I ended up doing a double major in zoology and agriculture. I had planned on taking an extra year in physical education, which would have allowed me to avoid teaching courses I didn't enjoy (like Latin), but then I fell ill with the mumps and had to forfeit all physical activity. As a result, I was forced to change directions.

I didn't know what to do, so one of my professors, knowing of my interest in lab tests and microscopes, suggested graduate work in pathology. Following her advice, I ended up at the University of Western Ontario. I began examining the effects of high blood pressure using a fluorescence microscope, a brand new invention. Soon I moved on to study the nervous system. I realized the heart was not an organ that intrigued me as much as the brain. A lot more secrets are buried up there. It was something I could be passionate about.

Then, having completed those studies, I began looking for a doctoral program. I was drawn towards the science behind vision, understanding how and what people see. My plan was to combine my work on the brain with ophthalmology — the study of the eyes.

Vision is essentially about the way you co-ordinate your eyes and how you're able to see an image clearly in three-dimensional depth. If there's a problem in one eye, it can give you double vision. Ophthalmology, as a discipline, failed to appreciate the connection between diseases in the eye and the entire nervous system. When people are in a coma, you can pinpoint the area of the brain that has been damaged simply by looking at how the eyes move. My goal was to combine our knowledge of what goes on at the front of the eye with what it's attached to at the back.

Space

My eyes had always been integral to my understanding of the world. As a child, I loved to lie on my back and look up at the clear night sky over Lake Superior, asking my parents to point out the different constellations. Influenced by the new space programs of the 1950s, I would stare at the vast expanse and imagine all the wild things that could be going on in outer space.

I also had an interest in flying. It must have come from my uncle, who was a part-time pilot. One Christmas when I was a child, he convinced my parents to let him take me up in his plane. I sat on his knees and we flew around the countryside. It was an incredible experience. In my third year of university, I tried taking lessons, but when I got the mumps, it paralyzed my arm and made it impossible to pull back the throttle.

Before I decided to become an astronaut, my scientific career had been all over the map — from zoology and agriculture to pathology and neurology. Because my mind moves in different directions very quickly, I have a tendency to get restless. The thing I learned, while moving from one domain to the next, was never to close doors behind me. I still managed to take courses that were general enough so that if I ever wanted to study medicine, for example, I would have the necessary prerequisites.

It wasn't until a little later that my urge to move into a completely new domain manifested itself. I was doing work at a neurology clinic in Boston on a scholarship when I learned that the *Columbia* space shuttle had landed. It had been the first shuttle flight. I snuck into the clinic in order to watch the coverage — it was the only place with a television — while pretending to do some paperwork. I was fascinated.

Two years later, I was in my car after finishing some clinic work when I heard an ad on the radio saying the Canadian space program was accepting applications — from men *and* women! I nearly drove into the ditch. I pulled off to the side of the highway and wrote down the information.

I think I was the second person to apply. I had to complete the application during my lunch breaks because I didn't want anyone at the clinic to know what I was doing. After a couple of weeks, I hadn't heard back and they put out another radio ad. I called in, sweating, thinking I had been turned down. "No," someone told me. "We just wanted more applicants."

Eventually, I was selected along with nineteen others to compete for one astronaut position. When I looked at the group, I knew they were going to hire me, not because I was the only woman, but because I was equal to the task. I had done the most schooling. Communication and people skills were at the forefront of their criteria. I had plenty of both, which was rare for candidates with the requisite scientific experience. I was extremely confident because I had been given the chance to compete for something I had always dreamed of.

The Most Important Thing

I have been many things in my career: an academic, a researcher, a teacher, as well as Canada's first female in space. My most important achievement, however, was becoming a physician. It has allowed me to save the lives of both my parents and is something I continue to do.

An astronaut has a very specific position in society. After going into space, I became a role model of sorts. I was a pioneer, someone who helped the field evolve technologically. But when it comes down to what I value

> *I'm probably the only person at our management consulting company who never took a university economics class. I did a BA in sociology. I was always very entrepreneurial, but, to me, getting a business degree seemed like getting a degree in plumbing. I figured I could pick it up pretty quickly on my own. I was interested in too many other things.*
>
> *In the year after undergrad, I wanted to do one of three things: drive a truck around North America, run an all-jazz radio station, or shadow a business leader. Because trucking required too much training and the local station didn't give me enough work, I settled on the third option and convinced the head of a chemical fertilizer company to create a "special projects" position for me and bring me on as a problem solver. I was basically a consultant. When I learned that people could actually move from a chemical company to a media company to a branch of the government, learning industries back-to-front and making recommendations, I was hooked.*
>
> *But that didn't stop me from doing a PhD in the philosophy of music.*
>
> — **David Pecaut**, senior partner at the Boston Consulting Group and Chair of the Toronto City Summit Alliance

most, it's the ability to ease suffering in others, to make someone else's life more comfortable. When I'm on my deathbed, looking back, I'll only consider myself a success if I've made a change in people's lives and if they remember me for how I helped them. As long as I'm not put into a box and forgotten — that would be my legacy. It's about being able to say, "Yeah, I had a good life — and it wasn't just for me."

"It's much better to do a very small thing right than a big exciting thing wrong."

Bruce Mau grew up near Sudbury, Ontario. Reacting against the environment of his youth, he has spent a career trying to develop new understandings of media and society. He is one of Canada's most noteworthy and internationally renowned designers. Massive Change, the project he instigated in 2005, took the country by storm and toured extensively throughout the world.

His vision of design, combining consumerist and postmodernist philosophy in equal measure, infuses all his work — including his design direction for Zone Books, his myriad branding projects, his controversial magazine pieces, and the jarring juxtapositions of his installations. Though hotly debated, Mau has, without a doubt, given electroshock therapy to North America's cultural landscape. He is currently in residence at the Art Institute of Chicago's architecture department.

"Put the Work First"

I owe a lot to a man by the name of Jack Smith. He was a teacher in Sudbury who taught me art in my last year of high school. The program involved colour photography, typography, ceramics, and anything else we could dream up. Because I had already taken the necessary credits, the entire year was dedicated to art alone. It was awesome: the most incredible time of my life.

Jack Smith was sixty-five years old and in his last year of teaching. The reason he was so effective was that he was manipulative. He would constantly put pressure on us and then prevent us from going forward, which had the result of inspiring us even more. When he went home, he would leave the door to the art room slightly ajar, so we could sneak in to work on our projects. He complained endlessly because I was always pressing him to do more. It was all part of a plan to instill in us a passion for art; I only realized that much later.

I was working on a piece one day — it happened to be Father's Day — and he came in to help. "Shouldn't you be with your family?" I asked. "No," he said. "I'd rather be here." I then told him how anxious I was that the year was about to end and that I couldn't imagine having that kind of experience again. He told me never to worry, to simply put the work first, focus on using the best of my capabilities, and everything else would line up: the money, the opportunities, interesting people to work with. "Don't get distracted," he said.

Art School

Until college, I had never really seen the world. In fact, I'd never been outside of Sudbury. I had become quite alienated by the general cultural sensibility there, which involved the classic Canadian stuff: hockey, drinking, and fighting. I had another orientation, knowing that I was going to live differently than the people around me. I didn't exactly know how, but I needed to make things happen in whatever way possible.

Television played an important role in my realization. Sitting in Sudbury watching documentaries, I could see there was a whole world out there that was nothing like the environment I knew. Almost no one my age was interested in art, media, and culture. I needed to get out. Luckily, the work I did with Jack Smith got me into art school in Toronto.

Coming to a big city and being enrolled at the Ontario College of Art was like blowing the doors off life. The artwork hanging in the school seemed so crazy to me. The students, thrilled to be accepted, had the ambition to do a million different things. I got to meet young women who actually wanted to be artists. There was even a transsexual in the waiting room when I had my interview. I was completely mesmerized. The categories had melted.

Much of what I learned there was similar to what Jack Smith had taught. I missed the opportunity of taking my work to the next level. Instead, I assumed I had to start at the beginning again. Classes became quite boring. The highs I felt from being around my fellow students were matched by the lows of dealing with classroom routine. I had thought I was at an art school but soon realized the "school" aspect was dominant. There was an administration, it was bureaucratic, and there were rules. The purpose became more about sustaining the institution than sustaining the vision. The fact that art was being created there seemed almost inconsequential.

On Display

I produced a lot of my own work, beyond the class requirements. It didn't fit with what teachers were asking of us. I remember one teacher looking at a painting of mine and saying, "No one will ever buy that." Though I agreed with him, it was not the most overwhelming response. When it came to the mid-year show, instead of displaying my class drawings, I innocently put up my personal pieces. Before the opening, the chairman of the school found out and was apparently furious. I heard around the school that I'd better lie low because he was looking for me.

The same day, a well-known journalist from New York came to lecture us. His presentation was on the work he had done for the *New York Times* about the cruelty of mental institutions; it was incredibly moving. "That's what we're here for," I remember telling one of my good friends. "That's exactly what I want to do with my work." While I went home to change for the opening, the writer took a tour of the school and was especially taken by my exhibit, telling the teachers I had talent. That evening, when I walked into the department, the chairman came up and, instead of reprimanding me, reached his hand out and said, "How ya doing, star?"

I was totally perplexed, looking around to figure out if he was really talking to me. Only two hours earlier, he had been out to get me. Then he explained what had happened. At first, I was really proud, but then I realized that if it took someone from New York to tell them what was interesting, their judgment was worthless. I was in the wrong place.

Working at Fifty Fingers

A local designer bought some drawings from the show. He was about to leave his job at a small design company called Fifty Fingers and recommended my work to them. When I went in for an interview, they were very positive. "We love your drawings," they said, "but can you design things?" I didn't know that much about it, but I thought I could give it a shot. I may have come across as arrogant, but it was ignorance more than anything — I had no idea what I was getting into. They offered me a job and I took it. A month later, I left art school and began working in design full-time.

Fifty Fingers, based in a former piano factory, was a young, hip design company. The work we did was pretty diverse, from artwork for the music business to corporate promotional material. I worked in one of the old clerical offices between two accomplished senior designers. Even though I was hired as a junior, I felt like I was on their level. We had three offices in a row with glass partitions and holes through which the clerks used to pass bills. We each had big drafting tables and would spend our days sitting and talking to each other through the holes, sending ideas back and forth. They were both fantastic influences on me. One was Swiss and the other was British. I became interested in the systematic dimensions of the Swiss and the humanistic dimensions of the British, wanting to bring the two sensibilities together. It was a perfect balance of science and aesthetics.

A Political Turn

At the time, the mentality in Toronto was that the world ended once you drove past Mississauga. There was a belief that all design, advertising, and journalism had to come from people in your city. Luckily, I was fortunate enough to work with some senior designers who taught me to think beyond boundaries. They told me not to be put off by closed-mindedness. If there was anyone in the world I wanted to work with, I should just go and talk to them. Everyone in the creative fields is the same: in search of work to develop their art.

As a result, after a few years at Fifty Fingers, I decided to move to England with an illustrator friend of mine. We found a place in London and I started to work for a design company. If my time in Toronto had taught me about design, art, and culture, being in England during the Thatcher years taught me about the world of politics. It was one of the worst periods in recent British history. They were at war in the Falklands, there were millions of homeless people, and there was staggering unemployment. You couldn't be apolitical.

In Canada, we're so sympathetic with the state that the state and our ambitions are sort of interwoven. In England, the conflict was both harsh and visible. You could see the state exerting its power and its effect on the citizens. People had to fight back, and it was quite incredible. Being in London when a million people marched together in protest was one of the most moving experiences of my life. It gave me a lot of faith in people.

I had the idea of trying to capture the political experience and insert it into the design world. Though I wasn't quite able to see how they could come together, it was something I believed in and wanted to bring about for the benefit of society. Two old art school friends, who were having a similar experience in New York, contacted me and asked if I wanted to start a company based on those ideals. I went to visit them and we planned the whole thing in New York. I quit my job in London and we all moved back to Toronto to found Public Good.

The Company

At that time there were hardly any non-governmental organizations around. There was the Red Cross and that was about it. There were a few organizations interested in literacy and health, but principally, all development work was done by the government. Public Good became the first of its kind. We set the agenda for taking design out of its narrow boundaries. The three of us formed a partnership and divided our tasks: a writer, a strategic thinker, and a designer. We did work, for instance, with the Ontario Nursing Association, and it involved much more than simply designing brochures. We were working on communication: with the doctors, the hospital, the public, and within the organization.

We began to develop the idea of branding, which dealt with understanding the message — the piece of information — that was being sent to the public. In the first couple of years with Public Good, these issues began to boil. We understood that at the stylistic heart of decision-making was design. When you look at a cup, you think the design is its shape. What we learned was that the shape is the least important part; the essence of its design is the flow of material that lets the cup come to you at a particular moment. Where does its material come from, how is energy applied to it, what kind of intelligence is necessary in the process? We went from thinking of design as a discrete thing to understanding it as an incredibly complex process.

This theory came from the ability to see the bigger picture. We live our lives like fish in a river. Every day you need to flow through and experience that river. Once in a while, however, you need to stand on the riverbank to see where it's all heading. At Public Good, we would spend entire days on the riverbank, trying to articulate the context and understand what was happening in the water.

Not everyone agreed with us. The great thing about Public Good was that it was like putting up a flag. Once you put it up, it was hard to take down. People from all over saw our name and wondered how a simple design business could be involved with the good of the public. They either hated us and turned away or they agreed with us and

Success for me didn't have anything to do with how big the company got or how much money we made. Success had much more to do with reaching my dreams. My driving force was always innovation and the creation of new machinery.

When young entrepreneurs approach me for advice, I always respond in the same way. "What's your hobby?" I'll say. "Pick your hobby and that is what you want to do. Don't go after the money. Go after what you love. The money will come as a fringe benefit."

— **Robert Schad**, founder of Husky Injection Molding Systems Inc.

began to adopt our philosophy. It had a polarizing effect, which galvanized us even more.

Security and Risk

One of the most common questions I get asked is about the pathway from my beginnings to where I am now. Young people want to be designers but they don't necessarily see the bridge. It seems like it requires a giant leap and the difficulty is in breaking it into incremental parts. What can an art student do today?

I think it all comes back to Jack Smith. I can still hear his voice from twenty-five years ago: focus on the work and let everything else fall into place. If you lay out the history of the studio with its ups and downs along the way, you see that it has always been about the same idea. I always worked hard and that's what projected me to the next day. It's much better to do a very small thing right than a big exciting thing wrong. You have to calibrate your whole life around working quietly and accepting compromises. I had to live like a student until five years ago, renting an apartment above a shop and being very modest with money. The challenge of Jack Smith's idea is that it's hard to know what the right work is in the present tense. One thing you have to accept is that security and stability are long-term achievements. You can't have them on a short-term basis. You need risk and instability in order to have the long-term effects. If you can't accept that, you're never going to get anywhere.

"I always believed it was a form of insanity to expect different results if we did the same thing over and over again."

When he was six, **Matthew Coon Come** was taken away from his family in Northern Quebec and sent to a residential school. While playing in the bush near his parents' tent-frame house, he heard a water plane land in the middle of a nearby lake, and before he knew it, he was apprehended by an RCMP officer and brought on board. He spent the next ten years at a boarding school run by the Anglican Church. Forbidden to retain the traditions of his Cree heritage, he was forced to learn an alien language and an alien culture. The whole time, he felt punished for something he had done wrong.

Later, after a degree from Trent University, he dropped out of McGill law school to return home and become chief of his band. As leader, he was able to challenge many development projects, both by Hydro-Québec and private business, that threatened to tread on Cree land. Because of people like him, industrial activities in the North cannot go forth without consultation with the affected aboriginal communities. Between 2000 and 2003 he was the national chief of the Assembly of First Nations. His success is attributable to a double-sided approach: being passionate about each cause and doing things differently from those who have come before.

Disappearing Forests, Rivers Flowing Backwards

My first run-in with political issues came when I was at high school in Hull, Quebec. Someone handed me a newspaper in which I read about Premier Robert Bourassa's intent to use the lakes around Rupert River as reservoirs for a massive construction project. Looking at a map, I realized this was land that belonged to my community. I started asking myself questions — "Was I going to be allowed home?" "What would happen to our area?" — and doing research on the issue. I soon learned that a large fraction of our land would be flooded and that my father, who was a hunter, would be forced out.

My people needed that land. In many ways, the land was the largest employer of our region because it allowed them — through fishing, hunting, and growing — to provide for themselves. These were isolated communities that didn't even have access roads until years later. I understood that the Rupert River project was going to drive the people off the land, forever displacing them and affecting their way of life.

It made me think of a story I was told about my grandmother. One day, while she was living out on the land, she went down to the lake to get a pail of water. While she was there, she looked over at a nearby mountain and saw the trees being eaten away. She looked at the mouth of the river and saw that the river was flowing backwards. And as she brought her pail into the water, she said to herself, "I'm going to pay for this one day."

When I stood by the same river, I saw the trees on the mountain being clear-cut by mechanized forest operators and I realized that the Government of Quebec was making the rivers flow backwards too. We were living out my grandmother's vision. That's what drove me to try and change things.

Learning the White Man's System

While I was at school, the idea of preserving our way of life was always in the back of my mind. One day, I talked to my father about it. "I'm not sure what I'm going to do," I said. "But once I've finished my schooling, I want to be in the bush with you."

"No," he said. "I will teach you, but I want you to go back to school. Learn from the white man's books, for we might use it against him."

"Why should I waste my time learning that?"

"Son, remember when I took you out on the land? If you know the land, and you know the behaviour of the animal, you know not to follow the tracks it leaves in the snow. You take shortcuts. You know where the lake is, so you go to the spot that he'll be running by in a few seconds. You'll know how the animal thinks and you'll be able to catch him."

If I knew how the government worked, I would be able to attack it. I followed his advice and decided to find out how the administrative machinery worked, how the Privy Council worked, and how the House of Commons made laws. I was going to learn the white man's system.

Lost Traditions

I went to Trent University and joined the Native Association. There were about sixty students in the organization, coming from across Canada — from Ontario, from Saskatchewan, from the Yukon. It was incredible meeting all these members of different groups. I was very involved, and despite being one of the youngest students, I became president of the organization.

We put on a number of events, from hosting the first annual elder's conference to throwing the best parties on campus. One year, we organized a canoe trip in Algonquin Park. I was leading the pack of about twenty with a friend of mine, setting up campsites and preparing the canoes. That's when I first realized the impact the residential schools had had on our way of life. We were at the front of six or seven boats paddling down the river when we came to a waterfall. Our boat went over, but when we looked back, we saw the others didn't know how to paddle; they were going around in circles. It made us chuckle, but we realized we'd have to teach them how to pack a canoe in a balanced way, how to paddle, and how to use the pole when going over rapids. It was a real eye-opener for these students. We taught them things about the land they'd never known.

A Call to Serve

While at McGill law school, I was continually intrigued and challenged. It had to do with my willingness to be coached, to be taught, to sit at somebody's feet who was smarter than I was. I didn't believe in hanging out with people who were my age: I would learn nothing. If I was with people who knew more, then it rubbed off on me. Sitting in lectures and listening to professors fit well with my personality.

I also became increasingly concerned about the issues affecting Native people across the country. I learned about treaty relationships, the recent court cases in our favour, and the agreements between the Crown and aboriginal peoples, which were known as land claims. I never understood the term "land

Soon after I immigrated to Canada, a relative of mine found me a job in a lumber mill beside the Fraser River in British Columbia. I worked there for a year and a half, pulling lumber off a grain train. Most of the workers came from India and I immediately felt a kinship with them. Some of them didn't speak much English and required interpretation and assistance. I eventually helped them organize a union. I've always felt closer to the underdogs in society. You can take the side of the rich and powerful, but there's not much fun in doing that. I always believed that it was the underdog who needed my assistance.

— **Ujjal Dosanjh**, premier of British Columbia, the first of Indian origin, 2000–01, and federal minister of health, 2004–06 claim": we had been living on the land for hundreds of years; who exactly were we claiming it from?

During my second year, an election was called back in my community. I was in the middle of writing exams when some of the elders of my band asked me if I wanted to run. There were eighteen other people nominated; I didn't think my chances were that strong. It was a difficult decision: as band chief, there was no salary, only an honorarium of $200 a month; if I finished law school and became a lawyer, I would make a lot of money, which I could send back to the community. The pull was strong. I consulted my father and other trustworthy people. In the end, the incumbent chief claimed he was stepping down in order to allow young people into leadership positions. It was an important declaration. The elders were now letting their children, the ones who had gone to school, take over. The shift in the direction of the community was enough to convince me that I needed to play a part.

The Election

In the end, I only had to run against one other person. I dropped right out of law school (never to return) and went up north to give my first speech. The community hall was packed. I arrived late, after my opponent had already spoken, and saw the faces of everyone in the community — my grandfather, my father, my uncle — everyone who I respected in this world. I was just a kid of twenty-four and here I was presenting my ideas to them.

I began by talking about the stories my grandfather used to tell me, as I sat with him by the riverbank, and the important role he played as a hunter. Then I spoke about the proposed activity in forestry and mining in our area, that our lakes would be used for reservoirs. And I proposed a plan. We could work on having our own structures, our own entities, and we could govern ourselves and manage our own businesses. We could re-examine our financial arrangements and bring capital into our community. We could control our land and resources and improve our standard of living to ensure long-term prosperity. I talked about possibility, co-operation, and commitment — and the crowd loved it.

Spreading the Word

I won the election and went to work right away. We weren't being consulted on activities in mining, forestry, or hydroelectric power, even though they affected us. One of our big initiatives was to oppose the Great Whale River Project, a plan by the Government of Quebec to dam some of our rivers for hydroelectric power. We had already participated in the parliamentary process, appeared before both federal and provincial committees, participated on energy boards, done presentations at universities, and debated the energy policy with Hydro-Québec. Many people thought we should give up because there was nothing we could do to stop the project. One day I woke up and asked myself, "Who is buying this energy anyway?" I realized the buyers were from the United States.

We went down to New York because Governor Mario Cuomo had signed a power agreement with Hydro-Québec. We arrived in Plattsburg, booked our talk at a church, and called everyone we knew, thinking we were going to make a huge impact. When I came on stage in the church basement, there were only eight people. At first, we were very disappointed. I had expected to be talking to a packed football stadium, debating on public talk shows, and meeting with the governors of all the northern states. Then I realized it was still a great opportunity. I tried to encourage the others. "Remember when we were kids. We would throw pebbles into the lake and create ripple effects." They didn't know what I was talking about. "Let me explain," I said. "Notice these eight people? They'll go home and their spouses will ask, 'Hey honey, how come you're late tonight?' And they'll say, 'There's this young chief from somewhere up near James Bay who was talking about losing his land.' Maybe they tell five people. Those five people will then tell another five people."

I learned that if you want to do something, you have to have a passion for it. My passion was for preserving a way of life for my people. I believed we had rights and that it was wrong to displace us. I believed there were alternatives to hydro energy and I dared to challenge the powers that be, to stand up for what I believed in. The key was to just keep pushing on.

Succeeding in the Struggle

Change does come about. We began challenging development projects with a multi-channel approach. We would have a political strategy, a legal strategy, an economic strategy, and a media campaign. We would educate ourselves about the organization we were taking on — how many vice-presidents they had, what kind of business structure they operated. Again, the key was learning their system and using it against them. It worked: the Government of Quebec has begun seriously looking into alternative sources of energy, such as wind power. Part of the reason came from our lobbying. We were the generation that had seen the horrible impact of the first hydroelectric developments and we weren't going to allow it to happen again.

We have made a difference by offering new ways of involving indigenous people in the business and government decision-making process. I always believed it was a form of insanity to expect different results if we did the same thing over and over again. You have to think outside the box. I would look around at what others were doing and I would do the opposite. Why do the same thing if it didn't work before?

If you can present something you have a passion for, people will usually rally around. If you can give them a mental picture of what the issue is, people will be even more willing to help. And if you can give them the feeling of making your fight their fight, your struggle their struggle, then you succeed. You'll have your critics; you'll have your supporters. But at the end of the day, if you don't give up, you can make a difference. Man made laws — man alone can change them.

YANNICK NÉZET-SÉGUIN

"Those first years were the hardest. It took determination, imagination, and a bit of craziness too."

Yannick Nézet-Séguin is the young star conductor of the Orchestre Métropolitain du Grand Montréal. Having committed himself to the study of music at a very early age, he has risen through the ranks of conducting at a *presto* pace. After graduating from Quebec's Conservatory of Music, he began conducting the choir of the Opéra de Montéal at twenty-three and was hired by the Orchestre Métropolitain as chief conductor at twenty-five. For the 2008–09 season, he will take his talent to the world stage as music director of the Rotterdam Philharmonic Orchestra.

Now in his early thirties, he has conducted all of his favourite operas and symphonies, from *Faust* to *Eroica*, in many of the world's great concert halls. His early success has much to do with specialization: other than piano, he has never learned a single instrument. As one capable of conducting all nine of Beethoven's symphonies from memory, he focuses his energies on being a conductor rather than a musician or a composer. "I'm not a genius," he says. "I'm an interpreter."

Prehistory

From very early on, I knew exactly what I wanted to do. If other people were deciding what to do in life at the age of twenty, I was doing it at ten. I knew then that I wanted to be a conductor.

Even though I began piano lessons when I was five, music didn't become serious until I was put in a church choir a few years later. The moment that vocals were added to piano and they came together in a choir, I was comfortable. At the same time, Charles Dutoit, the conductor of the Orchestre Symphonique de Montréal, was becoming a big star in the media. I went to one of his concerts and was so fascinated that I started drawing the orchestra. Even before I knew how to conduct, I wanted to capture the feeling — even visually — of a symphony.

Though my family was never particularly musical, they believed in instruction. My grandparents had been teachers, as well as my father. Pedagogy was important. So, while I continued with the choir, I also started taking classes at the conservatory. Both those pursuits were very important to my development as a conductor. I learned that, as much as I strive for things, I should always transmit what I know to others. That applied especially to the choir, which I was able to start conducting in rehearsals when I was thirteen.

Further Studies

Throughout my adolescence, it was hard to balance music with academic studies. In primary school, I was a good student. Around the age of fifteen, I began to realize that my interest in music would seriously limit my chances of doing well at school. I made a conscious decision to focus on music, not school. It became difficult to deal with the attitudes of others. No one thought a career in music was possible. It wasn't seen as safe. My parents, thankfully, were not of that mindset.

Unfortunately, my high school refused to give me equivalence credits for the courses I was doing at the conservatory. That annoyed me because I had to work twice as hard to keep up both aspects. I spent the week at school and weekends at the conservatory. If I wanted to practise piano, I had to do it at night. Today, looking back, I'm grateful. If you're given permission, it's too easy. To succeed, you need to be committed. A musician's schedule is always difficult. There have to be sacrifices — though it's important to remember they aren't considered sacrifices if you truly love what you're doing.

My academic studies also gave me a broader view of the world. I developed an interest in the humanities, especially history and psychology. As a conductor, this has helped me enormously. When I conduct a symphony, for example, I need to know how it relates to history: what does Beethoven's *Eroica* have to do with Napoleon? What kind of rhetoric is being used by the composer? What kind of society is being reflected? Psychology is another important tool. It helps me understand the mindset of the characters I'm directing in an opera, as well as the musicians I have to lead. I need to know how they function, how they react, and how I can get the best out of them.

Building a Reputation

Once I finished CEGEP at eighteen, I was able to devote myself entirely to conservatory studies. I graduated from piano at twenty-one, then, at twenty-two, I did the equivalent of a master's in chamber music.

Around that time, I founded a performance ensemble with two other conservatory members. We called it La Chapelle de Montréal. It may have been thoughtless, but the idea was to put on concerts, convince other young people to get involved, and keep it going for two years. The profits would be split evenly for everyone involved and we'd each make no more than $75 a show. I wanted to do it because, even though I'd had some experience conducting my church choir, I needed to see if I was able to conduct instruments as well. That was a crucial requirement of my development.

After we had recruited enough musicians, we began putting on concerts. At first, the venues were all churches, which were lent to us cheaply because I had sung at some of their religious services. It was always difficult to get people's respect. Luckily, for our first show, we had articles in *Le Devoir*, *The Hour*, and *La Presse*. The media appreciated our musical ambition. The first piece we did was J.S. Bach's *Saint John Passion*, which was not often performed. The thought that twenty-year-olds were attempting it got people's attention. Afterwards, we concentrated on doing other less-performed works. We had to survive without making money for two years before we could create a board and begin asking the government for subsidies. Those first years were the hardest. It took determination, imagination, and a bit of craziness too.

While the concerts gave me some practice and showed the critics I was professional, I still needed to see how an experienced conductor worked. I got the idea of doing something even more ambitious. Having always been an admirer of the great conductor Carlo Maria Giulini, I wrote a letter to his office in Milan and asked if I could study with him. I didn't hear back, so, being a little stubborn, I wrote again. Then I left for a piano competition in Europe. I happened to be in Trieste, Italy, when my parents phoned to say he had faxed back. I was so excited. I called him and we spoke. He said he could not teach me conducting: I either had the ability or I didn't. I took the train to Milan and met with him. I told him I didn't want to be taught; I just wanted to attend his rehearsals and concerts. To this, he responded very generously.

I ended up spending one year with him and following his orchestra around Europe. I was still living in Montreal, but I took seven transatlantic trips. I went with them to Milan, Paris, Turin, Switzerland, and Spain. His orchestra would

> *If I had a broken foot and was asked to play, they'd take the cast off, tape it up, and I'd play. If you want to accomplish something, you just do it. Don't complain and don't wait for someone to push you along the way. If you want to get in shape, you get in shape. Somebody cracking the whip is not going to do it for you.*
>
> — **Red Kelly**, eight-time Stanley Cup winner with the Detroit Red Wings and the Toronto Maple Leafs and Liberal Member of Parliament for York West, 1962–65

rehearse, then I would sit down with him and talk. Once every trip, we'd even go to his house near Milan and discuss passages that had intrigued me.

It may sound trite, but luck is an important element of success. You have to create your chances, take your opportunities, and make the most of them; but, in the end, it comes down to being at the right place at the right time. I created my chance by writing to Giulini, and because I happened to be in Italy when he wrote back, I was able to say yes. I was also lucky enough to catch him in his last year of active conducting. He retired shortly afterwards.

The Big Break

When I finished my year with Giulini, I got a phone call from the Opéra de Montréal: they wanted to interview me for a job. They knew about my work with the ensemble and my apprenticeship in Europe because someone had passed on my CV. Even though I never officially applied, they hired me as choirmaster. The job involved rehearsing the choir before each opera and, often, conducting it from off-stage during the show. It was a great experience because it also allowed me to see how an orchestra worked.

Two years later, the Orchestre Métropolitain du Grand Montréal offered me a job as conductor and I was in a good position to accept. There were still many difficulties because, since I was only twenty-five, a lot of the board members were skeptical. But others said, "He has put on his own concerts. Critics approve. He can draw a full house. He planned seasons, got subscriptions, and found musicians." That was exactly what they needed for a conductor. Not just someone to wave a stick around, but also someone to plan ahead and manage the administrative side. I had created my chance; now I was given an opportunity to be at the head of a great symphony orchestra.

Getting a job as a musician can be rigorous. They audition you from behind a curtain, it's all done by number, and everyone gets the same treatment. For a conductor, it's more complicated. There has to be chemistry. When I was hired, the Orchestre Métropolitain knew I could work with the musicians, many of whom I had conducted before. I was also able to deal with the responsibility of hiring the choir, planning the season, and dealing with the board of directors. They had to know I could connect with them. It went far beyond what was on my CV.

"I cooked by feel and by memory. I didn't work from a book."

Rob Feenie has been at the forefront of a culinary revolution in Canada. When he started his career at Vancouver's Dubrulle Institute at the age of twenty, English Canada was still largely unfamiliar with fine dining and haute cuisine. After ten years of intense training, Feenie established Lumière Restaurant in Vancouver and raised the bar for international cooking in the country. In November 2000, Lumière was the first freestanding Canadian restaurant to receive the Relais Gourmand designation. Since then, Feenie has opened two other Vancouver establishments, overhauled Le Régence in Manhattan, established the Accolade Restaurant in Toronto, published three cookbooks, and begun hosting *New Classics with Rob Feenie* on the Food Network. He is also one of the few people ever to have won a battle against Iron Chef Masaharu Morimoto on *Iron Chef America*.

While weekday meals in Feenie's childhood home were rushed affairs, his parents always ensured that Sunday dinner was a special occasion. On Sundays, the Irish-Canadian family's table was piled high with roasts, vegetables, and Yorkshire pudding. But it wasn't until Feenie's exchange trip to Sweden at the age of fifteen that he discovered the culinary world extended beyond such standard fare.

Opening My Eyes

Growing up, the only travelling I did was for hockey tournaments in Seattle. I always read and dreamed about visiting more exotic places. Canada wasn't nearly as multicultural back then. Now, you can walk down the street and see and taste the world, but in the early 1980s, that wasn't the case. One day, a girl came to our high school to talk about the Rotary International Exchange Program. She had spent a year in Germany and her stories had me spellbound. I signed up immediately, went through the interview process, and ultimately got chosen. When I did, they asked me to fill out my first three countries of choice. I chose Sweden first, France second, and Japan third. I have no idea why I chose Sweden, but I did and that's where they sent me.

The program placed me with a family in Gothenburg, right on the ocean, forty-five minutes from Stockholm. They lived in a gorgeous house with a huge back garden where they grew all kinds of vegetables. They took the freshness and quality of the food they ate very seriously. It became my job to run to the store and buy cheese and other delicacies. Gradually, I started doing a good deal of the cooking as well.

I got to go everywhere: Finland, Denmark, Germany, Austria, Northern Italy, France, and Belgium. I can still remember being hit by my first taste of Belgian fries and French cheese. I cook by taste — that's always what inspired me.

When I returned to Vancouver, I was a changed person. I wanted to be a part of the world I'd discovered. The only problem was that I didn't know how.

A "New" Profession

When I came home, the school board wanted me to do half of Grade 11 over again. As a result, I was suddenly behind all my friends. When I finished the year, the majority of the people I'd grown up with suddenly took off for university. I still had another year to decide if I would follow them. I wasn't sure that I wanted to.

During that time, I got a part-time job as a banquet waiter at a hotel that later became the Ramada Inn. As a waiter, I could pick up the things I had grown used to in Europe: fine coffee, cheese, and other ingredients. Around that time, I started cooking for fun and testing out things on my friends. I also started reading about food and collecting cooking magazines.

While I was at the hotel, I worked a function for the Chefs' Association of British Columbia. Pierre Dubrulle, who had just opened the Dubrulle International Culinary and Hotel Institute of Canada, was sitting at the table I was serving. I managed to sneak a brief chat with him and he gave me his card.

In Vancouver in the early 1980s, cooking wasn't respected as a profession. We had a few good cooks, but there weren't many fine dining restaurants. Gradually, though, that was starting to change. Wolfgang Puck was getting started in California and the buzz was spreading. You could feel that something was going to happen. After I served Pierre and took his card, I forgot all about going to university with my friends. I knew I wanted to cook — and I haven't looked back since.

The Dubrulle Institute

Though I had missed the school's first six-month program, I went down to Dubrulle and filled out an application. I was unbearably excited. I was only eighteen and chefs from Northern France and Italy were going to teach me to cook.

I had amazing teachers. One, from Northern Italy, was good friends with my mother, which allowed me to pull more information from him than the other students in the class. I would stay late and press him with question after question.

I had complete tunnel vision. I hardly paid attention to the other students in the program. Many of them were professional people who had day jobs in other fields. They enjoyed the process but few of them were really looking to make a career out of cooking. I was. I was eighteen years old, and for me it was all about the food. I pitied friends who had gone on to university to study things they weren't interested in. While I sometimes questioned whether I was making the most practical decision, I knew I loved what I was doing.

A Bit of Luck

I don't know what it is about life, but sometimes things come down to luck. Coming out of Dubrulle, I got incredibly lucky and got to work in all the places that I wanted to work. The first place was a little French restaurant that Pierre decided was the best place for me. I left school just as the chef was leaving to start his own restaurant. The restaurant must not have known what to make of me, but during my time there, I got my sea legs in a professional kitchen.

After that, another teacher at Dubrulle helped me get a job at the Rimrock Cafe and Oyster Bar in Whistler. He just phoned me up and said, "Bob Dawson owns the most successful restaurant in Whistler. I've talked to him and he wants you." Despite the concentration of restaurants in Whistler and the fierce competition, the Rimrock was always full. It was the model of a well-run, quality culinary enterprise.

Working as a sous-chef there not only helped me develop as a culinary artist but also taught me the business side of being a restaurateur. I went through a few rocky places after that, but my first two jobs were remarkable experiences. I couldn't have asked for a better start.

Staying on the Move

When you're starting out in the culinary business, it's important to move around; spend two years in one place, then move, spend three years in another, and then move again. Right now, I have a young cook of mine in London working for Gordon Ramsay. He's been there a year, and in another year, he'll leave. If he stays any longer, he'll burn out. But it's imperative to travel as much as you can while you're young. You need to work for as many top chefs as you can. You need to sample from as many different kitchens and chefs as possible. That way, when you get older, you'll have more of a repertoire to draw from.

I cooked by feel and by memory. I didn't work from a book. But when I cook, everything I've experienced in this business informs what I do, even if I'm unaware of it. The more experiences you have in different kitchens, in different countries, and under different circumstances, the richer the influences you'll bring to your own cooking.

Alsace

When I was eighteen, I told myself that I would have my own restaurant by the time I was thirty. When I was twenty-seven, I thought I was ready to go it alone. At the same time, I knew I probably needed more exposure to European cuisine. It's a good thing that I waited. I looked around at the Vancouver scene and honed in on Marc Jacob, who ran Le Crocodile. He was French, dexterous, and highly skilled. He was exactly what I needed, so I went and applied. Working at Le Crocodile opened my eyes to Alsatian cuisine and thus helped me see where I needed to go in the future.

After working for Marc for a little while, he sent me to Alsace to work with the man who had taught him how to cook. I stayed with Marc's mother and brother and lived the way I had lived with my exchange family in Sweden. The region and its food instantly got beneath my skin and into my blood. Its flavours permeated my soul. Alsace boasts one of the best wineries in the world in terms of white varietals. It's a magical place.

Marc's teacher was one of the greatest chefs I had ever met. He had two tiny places in Strasbourg, where I ate some of the best food I had ever tasted. He introduced me to an entire community of great chefs, including Émile Jung. I worked at Émile's restaurant — a Michelin three-star establishment — while I was in Alsace, which was a hugely influential experience.

When you go to Europe as a twenty-seven-year-old North American, they know that they can get you to work for free, but, to me, it never mattered that I wasn't paid. I was set up with a place to stay and I ate for free at the restaurants.

When I dropped out of grad school, I started teaching high school in Petrolia, Ontario. I was a horrible teacher, but I really enjoyed it. One summer, I planned a trip through Europe with a friend who was a senior lecturer at the University of Western Ontario. Because his school year finished earlier than mine, he took our money, went ahead, and blew it all. By the time I arrived in London, there was only $200 left from my original $640. Intent on visiting the Lapland in northern Norway, I set off to hitchhike to Scandinavia. After five weeks, I was just above the Arctic Circle when the road ended. I squandered my remaining money in a bar and had to live off blueberries for a few weeks as I made my way to the Canadian Embassy in Helsinki, where my mother could wire me more.

Desperate for funds when I got back to London, I took a teaching job in Essex, and then a job as a hall porter at the British Council's Overseas Student Centre. I had a wonderful time. I ran around town, hung out with foreign students, and loafed around Canada House reading the papers from back home. When I returned to Canada, I approached my teaching with a new maturity and seriousness, but my sense of adventure hadn't been satisfied. I wanted to see more of the world. That's when I applied for the Foreign Service.

— **James Bartleman**, former Canadian ambassador to Cuba, Israel, NATO, and the EU, and lieutenant-governor of Ontario, 2002–07

Working six days a week didn't give me much chance to spend money. As long as you can fly to where you're going, you can usually make it work. It would have been more difficult if Marc hadn't helped me out, but the experience of working in a European kitchen is so important that young chefs should do anything they can to get into one.

Starting a Restaurant

When I started talking about opening my own place while working at Le Crocodile, Marc Jacob thought I was insane. He was right. Opening your own restaurant is crazy no matter how old you are, but it's especially ridiculous when you're as young as I was. I was twenty-nine when I opened Lumière. When I started the financing for the restaurant, I didn't give any thought to whether opening it made good business sense. I just wanted to have a restaurant. That's all I could think about. I had given myself a timeline and I was determined to make it happen.

It was incredibly hard work, but I eventually found an initial business partner. I had a little bit of money of my own and a little from my parents, and with that last kick of financing, we had enough to get Lumière off the ground.

I'm very careful about recommending that young chefs take the same road I did. You need to be far more cautious and business savvy than I was. You need to devote a great deal of attention to finding the right location for your restaurant. Vancouver is far too saturated with restaurants right now. When I set up Lumière, there weren't many options in terms of fine dining, but that's changed completely. Whistler is a great example of how things can go wrong. New restaurants are opening there all the time and they're having a tough time financially. It's not enough to simply have the dream and the desire. You need to have a cool head and a solid plan to succeed.

The First Year

The first year of running Lumière was unbelievably hard, largely because I hadn't thought everything through. We opened in November 1995, and by October of 1996 things were so bad business-wise that I had to rethink my entire formula. I really owe the restaurant's survival to two people: Ken Wai, my business partner, and Charlie Trotter, a master chef from Chicago. In November 1996, I went down to do some training with Charlie. He helped me see that I should have confidence in my own voice as a chef. His food combined myriad elements — you could taste hints of Japanese, Italian, Chinese, French, and American influences. Working with him helped me see that I shouldn't be worried about letting my various culinary influences speak clearly. I wanted to make great French cuisine, of course, but I needed to free myself to cook by feel. I returned from Chicago with a clear head and new ideas. Luckily, Ken Wai believed in my instincts and threw in some more money to keep us afloat. I never thought about closing the doors, but I knew I needed to make changes.

Too often, people looked at my restaurant and said, "Wow, that guy must be unbelievably successful!" What they don't realize is how much work and expense goes into getting your restaurant on the map. I had to do lots of travelling and mingling, figuring out the best way to get acknowledged and to get the big boys in the culinary world to visit the restaurant. I had to go to Europe three to four times a year and that's not cheap. It took ten years for Lumière to become a real success as a business.

Why I Do It

In the beginning, I wanted to give the people who ate at Lumière the type of experience I'd had dining in Europe. I wanted to touch people with food.

My thinking about food has changed a thousand times over my career. I've conceptualized it with metaphor after metaphor, but over the last twenty years, I've learned that, in the end, the customer and their experience with the food is all that matters. Making food that gives customers a unique and powerful experience is remarkably hard. It takes an insane amount of work. I'm just arriving there now, I think, and it feels wonderful.

RAYMOND MORIYAMA

"Experience had taught me that architecture needed to be part of the surrounding landscape, in balance with a larger natural system."

Raymond Moriyama is one of the most respected and celebrated architects in Canada. After designing the Japanese Canadian Cultural Centre as a young man, Moriyama was launched into a prominent career, earning commissions to design the Ontario Science Centre, Sudbury's Science North, the Canadian Embassy in Tokyo, the National Museum of Saudi Arabia, and Canada's new War Museum in Ottawa. Known for their stunning simplicity and humility, Moriyama's buildings have always sought to respect and complement the natural environments in which they find themselves.

Moriyama claims his desire to be an architect began early. Having sustained a nearly fatal burn at the age of four, he was confined to his bed for months. He spent his days gazing out the window at a construction site across the street. To a child's eye, the men were building a palace, and the architect was larger than life. "I want to be an architect!" the four-year-old announced to anyone who would listen. Eight years later, after the bombing of Pearl Harbor, the Moriyama family lost their Vancouver hardware store and, along with hundreds of other Japanese Canadians, found themselves in an internment camp at Bay Farm, British Columbia. Self-conscious about his burn marks, Moriyama would slip down to a nearby river to bathe. It was there that he built himself a tree house — a perch from which to escape the troubles of the camp and to commune with nature. The experience taught him economy of scale and the need to harmonize with the surrounding environment. It also made him more keen to pursue architecture later in life.

Sticking Out like a Sore Thumb

When I arrived at the University of Toronto to study architecture, I was still relatively ignorant as to what would be involved or who the great architects were. I didn't even know what a sanding block was! Luckily, the technical aspects were easy to pick up. All that really mattered was that I had desire and vision.

Compared to the rest of the students in my program, I stuck out like a sore thumb. To most, "Contemporary Architecture" was god. Everyone knew and worshipped the big-name architects. They were interested in designing buildings that would leave a grand and distinct mark on the world. I didn't feel the same way at all. Experience had taught me that architecture needed to be part of the surrounding landscape, in balance with a larger natural system.

Building my tree house in the forest near Bay Farm had instilled in me a deep appreciation for harmony. Nature is capable of such a perfect balance of diverse elements when humans aren't around. I wondered why structures couldn't incorporate themselves into that balance rather than attempt to destroy it.

I lived in a consumer-based society, but I was never truly in tune with its values. "You don't have to move a mountain," my grandfather used to tell me as a child. "The truth can lie under the smallest pebble." I've always remembered and cherished that insight. Often, in professional circumstances, we say, "I'll move a mountain for you." We are always aiming to do things bigger and better. That impulse is a good one, but it often leads to monumental errors. Humility and clear-thinking go hand in hand.

Working with Dr. Arthur

The first assignment we were given was an essay on why we'd chosen to be architects. In my paper, I told the story of my tree house and briefly outlined my vision of how architecture should work. Dr. Eric Arthur, who was the dean of architecture, gave me an A+. He said it was the best explanation for being an architect he had ever read. After that, he took a shine to me.

In the summer after my second year, I was working at a construction site in Hamilton, Ontario — where my family now lived — when Dr. Arthur phoned me. "How would you like to come and work for me in Toronto?" he asked. I said no. The summer was the only time I could spend with my family. There was a silence before he answered. "What if I pay for your bus fare every day?" Again, I turned him down. Before he hung up, he told me to ask my father.

When I did, my father was irate. "Phone him back and tell him you'll take the job," he exclaimed. I phoned Dr. Arthur and told him my father had given me hell. He laughed and said he'd be thrilled to have me.

He ended up paying me very well and following through on his bus fare promise. On top of that, he gave me a room with a wonderful bay window, a drafting board, and a private bathroom. Dr. Arthur came in every morning and we would spend an hour talking about architecture. I learned an immense amount and, in a funny way, I think he even enjoyed our talks.

One day, it was after twelve and Dr. Arthur hadn't come in yet. I assumed he must have forgotten our meeting, so I decided to take a bath in my ensuite bathroom. As I lay in the tub, I heard the door squeak open and a voice whisper, "Ray? Ray? Are you there?" I told him I was busy, but he walked in anyway. He sat on the edge of the tub and started talking about column designs. Although it was an interesting conversation, I must say I felt a little uncomfortable. He stayed for an hour, then stood up and said, "Okay, see you tomorrow."

Learning from the Mistakes of Others

The next summer, I worked for an architect in Hamilton. He was a nice man but a terrible architect. I had always assumed that architects had integrity, a work ethic, and a dedication to the craft, but this guy was sloppy. For example, in his designs for one house, instead of outlining every stone in the facade, he drew a few scattered circles, wrote "stone," and assumed the builders would know what he meant. Of course, they built the house based on the drawings. Instead of a stone facade, there was only a peppering of stones across the front. The architect was furious, screaming at the builders for not following his designs. Actually, they had followed the drawings perfectly. The architect argued that the contractor should have known better. When I asked if he had ever been to the site, he said no.

By the end of the first few weeks, I was doing all the designing for him. It was great experience, but there's no way a professional firm should allow a third-year student to design schools and buildings. Working there taught me that you couldn't allow yourself to be lazy. Every detail matters.

Connecting Architecture and Experience

When I left the University of Toronto, I won a scholarship to McGill's master of architecture program. I was there to study town planning and civic design, but in the end I spent more time taking sociology, psychology, and anthropology classes. The only class I ever failed was in architecture. At the time, the study of architecture seemed too narrowly focused on design and construction. It didn't examine how societies worked, how people acted, and what kind of positive change the world was looking for. I wanted to think about the relationship between buildings and people, ethics and the environment. Since nobody was teaching that in the architecture faculty, I had to go out and learn what I could in other disciplines.

Starting a Business

When I left McGill at twenty-eight, I had the option to join an established firm. But I was a headstrong young man with ideas of my own and I wanted to take my own risks. I wanted to set up a firm. There were obvious challenges. To begin with, I was married with two children. Secondly, we only had $392 in the bank.

When I approached my wife, she surprised me. She was completely supportive. "Ray," she said, "the only thing that can go wrong is that you may have to go back and work for another architect. Go for it." She was wonderful! So I went for it. I set up my own firm on the second floor of a semi-detached house on Yorkville Avenue in Toronto. A large part of my office space had to be shared with another firm. My drafting board was a door laid across a couple of sawhorses.

It was very hard for my husband and me, newly arrived in India and both in our mid-twenties, to get anything started. Calcutta is a city built for 3 million but inhabited by 18 million. My husband befriended an old Muslim gentleman who owned a piece of property. They would have tea together. "My family is against it," the man would say. "I can't have a church next to my building when there's a mosque right across the street." Finally, he agreed to sell us the land and we were able to build the first church in Calcutta in a hundred years.

— **Huldah Buntain**, co-founder and senior pastor, Calcutta Mission for Mercy (pictured with her late husband, Mark)

Two days after the office opened, Joseph Crothers of the Crothers Construction Equipment Company phoned with a commission for kitchen cupboards. The next day, I received his cheque in the mail for $1,000. I was overjoyed. Suddenly, there wasn't as much pressure.

That first job initiated a long-term and fruitful relationship with the Crothers family, including commissions for everything from golf courses and private planes to the company's head office. The jobs were varied, but each one further cemented our relationship. The Crotherses appreciated my dedication and attention to detail. They also appreciated that no job was too small or insufficiently connected to my focus. We did everything. I'd stay up all night talking about minute little details. They appreciated that and spread the word.

The Japanese Canadian Cultural Centre

The Japanese Canadian Cultural Centre marked a serious turning point in my career. It focused on giving the Japanese-Canadian community strength and self-respect after many years of incarceration, injustice, and discrimination. It was about Canada, rooted deeply in Canadian soil and in the multicultural future of Canada. It also had to be inexpensive (the final cost was $14.14 per square foot), virtually prefabricated, and built in winter.

Over the years, we grew a little in size, but we didn't wish to grow just for the sake of growing. When we received a call from the minister of public works in 1964, six years later, I assumed they had the wrong number or were calling about a minor project. I told the minister I was too busy and hung up. When he phoned back and finally persuaded me to meet with him, I assumed the rendezvous would be a waste of time. When he asked me to design the Ontario Science Centre, I was astonished and refused the commission immediately. The minister was persuasive. "We are looking for a young architect with imagination, passion, and guts. That's you!" Wow. How could I refuse such a challenge? It was an offer to celebrate Canada's centennial and make a difference in science and technology, while balancing it with nature. I had to accept.

"Suddenly, I was getting to meet real people and experience something that didn't feel anaesthetized or packaged."

Bruce Poon Tip unwittingly helped create an industry. Before his first six-person trip to Ecuador in 1991, "eco-tourism" didn't exist. While backpacking through Thailand, Poon Tip realized that cruises and sanitized, resort-based vacations kept travellers away from the very things that made countries great: the people. As a result, he returned to Toronto and established G.A.P Adventures, a package travel company whose tours would take visitors off the beaten track and into local communities — leaving a minimal ecological footprint. Seemingly radical at the time, the model has had a huge impact on the mainstream travel industry. G.A.P Adventures is now a $120-million business, selling trips to more than a hundred eclectic destinations from twenty-seven representative offices worldwide. Only forty years old, Poon Tip has twice been honoured with the Canadian Entrepreneur of the Year Award.

It's easy to see how the Trinidad-born Poon Tip was no ordinary kid. By the age of sixteen, he had already run three successful businesses. Though he'd been fired from both Denny's and McDonald's within the same month, entrepreneurship came naturally. "I believed I could sell anything," he recalls with a smile. "I could have brought back the pet rock and made it a hit again." Leaving high school, Poon Tip was desperate to find a niche for himself and make a splash in the business world.

Born Selling

I was a natural entrepreneur. When I was twelve, I nabbed eight different newspaper delivery routes and subcontracted the labour to money-hungry friends who weren't old enough to work. It was a paper route ring. I'm sure it was highly illegal, but somehow the people in charge of the different areas never clued in that they had all hired the same person.

Two years later, I began importing Dutch dwarf rabbits into Canada. I had always been intrigued by the problem posed by the domestication of rabbits. People loved rabbits when they were young and cute but invariably handed them off to animal shelters when they grew big and awkward. One day, in a pavilion at the Calgary Stampede, I saw these Dutch rabbits that never grew. I thought, "Wow, I bet people would eat these up." When I discovered that no one was importing the rabbits into Canada, I got the breeders' contact information in the Netherlands, looked into the difficulties of importation, found a broker, and started a rabbit breeding business.

I had no clue about breeding rabbits, but gradually I learned. I didn't know, for example, that after babies are born the father tries to kill them. My first two rabbits — Tipper and Daisy — gave birth to a huge brood and I sold the babies to local pet stores. The demand was huge. Later, because my rabbits always won the competitions at local 4-H clubs, I started conducting stud services as well — which turned out to be even more profitable.

I wrote a book as well, called *The Caring of Dutch Rabbits*. The first copies were Duo-Tangs full of photocopied pages with a drawing of a rabbit on the front. The books were sold at local book and pet stores, and everyone who bought a rabbit bought a book.

The Business School Bust

When high school was finished, I started taking business courses at the University of Calgary and Mount Royal College (which wasn't yet part of the university). I found the whole experience underwhelming. Business school was grooming us all to work for IBM, and that's all the students seemed to want. Whenever representatives from big multinational corporations came in to give talks, the students would swoon as though they were meeting rock stars. The whole culture of business school was wrong for me. The prospect of working at IBM or General Foods left me cold.

The one thing that sparked my interest was an assignment we did on the tourism industry. After doing a fair amount of research, I created a business model for a company that ran off-the-beaten-track tours. I got a horrible grade. To the teacher, my business model made no sense. I wasn't convinced. Afterwards, I enrolled in a tourism management course at a local college, just to see how the industry worked. The course was interesting, and for a time I flirted with the idea of pursuing something in the tourism industry, but at that point, my thoughts hadn't really come together yet. I wasn't sure I knew what I wanted to do.

Instead of trying to paint professionally during my twenties, I taught high school, lectured on naturalism, and travelled around the world. I continued to paint in my free time, as I had done since I was a child. I never expected to support myself with my art. The work I produced was largely influenced by cubism and abstract expressionism. When I took drawing classes during university, my teacher taught me that if you couldn't draw something with the back of a broom, it wasn't worth painting. I wanted to be au courant, so for many years, I transformed my naturalist sketches of gulls and white-tailed deer into abstract paintings. I still don't regret that time. In many ways, abstraction underlies all of my work.

It wasn't until I was thirty-two years old that I had my "road to Damascus moment." It happened at an Andrew Wyatt show in Buffalo, New York. My travels had made me realize humanity was wiping out the world's natural diversity. To understand why things were worth saving required an appreciation of their uniqueness. Wyatt's paintings captured the particularity of things. His show inspired me to return to the more representative style I had used as a kid.

— **Robert Bateman**, world-renowned wildlife painter and naturalist

Taking a Chance

After those two years of fruitless study in Calgary, I picked up and moved to Toronto, aiming to start a business. I had never visited Toronto before, so I didn't have a clue what to expect. I arrived with $800, a college credit card, and a whole lot of piss and vinegar, but not a very clear clue as to what I was going to do.

My parents were not very happy with my choice. Neither were a lot of my friends. To them, I was turning my back on them. Few people could see that I needed to take a leap and try something new.

At the time, I thought I wanted to start a record label. I thought all the best bands were in Toronto, so I figured all I needed to do was to find a good one, manage it, and then build the label around them. Suddenly, Nirvana blew up and the entire music industry changed. I had been raised on corporate rock, U2, and The Smiths. That's the model I understood. The new, stripped down, four-track alternative rock threw the music industry into upheaval. I liked the new music, but I couldn't understand how to sell it, so I gave up on starting my own label and began searching for a new idea.

A Light Bulb on the Road

Not long after I arrived in Toronto, I decided to travel to Thailand with some old friends. I didn't have much money at the time, but it felt like the right thing to do and the right time to do it.

Thailand is where everything changed. I was living off less than $10 a day, staying with locals, doing the classic backpacker thing, and it suddenly occurred to me that this was the only way to travel. I was getting to meet real people and experience something that didn't feel anaesthetized or packaged. I was disgusted with the difference between my previous experience and my present one. I knew that there had to be enough people who wanted an alternative to sitting in the sun at a gated resort and avoiding the heart of the country.

There must be a company that duplicates the backpacker experience, I thought, and puts people into contact with local cultures. Before the Internet, there was no way for me to discover whether such a company existed. I asked travellers I met, but no one seemed to have heard of anything. When I returned to Toronto, I flipped through the Yellow Pages, but I wasn't even sure what to look for.

Before I had left for Thailand, I knew I needed to come home with a clear plan: would I stay in Toronto or return to Calgary? Suddenly, the answer was clear. If there wasn't a company like the one I could see in my mind's eye, then I would make one. I would stay in Toronto and do whatever it took to get the company off the ground.

Scouting the First Trip

I refer to the period that followed my return to Toronto as my "political phase." I was young and angry. I thought the norm in the tourism industry was sickening. I couldn't understand why, if given the choice, people would opt for something banal and lethargic rather than something authentic and challenging.

G.A.P was about more than starting a business; it was about an idea — one I thought was long overdue. The problem was that no bank would give me a loan. I guess the idea seemed loony to them. In the end, I had to finance the company with credit cards and the little money I had in savings from my old businesses.

The first thing I needed was a trip. After a heavy amount of research, I decided on Ecuador. It was perfect: there is perhaps nowhere else in the world where you can go from mountains like the Andes into rainforest and then to a place like the Galapagos Islands in a matter of days. The only problems were that I'd only been to Ecuador once and I was broke. Before I left on my scout trip, I mapped out precisely what I wanted to do. Then I flew in and tried to establish contacts on the ground. I remember meeting tribesmen up in the Andes and telling them that, in six months, a group of North Americans would need accommodation. They looked at me like I was insane.

Finally, I ran out of money. A friend of mine was coming to meet me in five days, but until then, I was a very hungry sitting duck. For those five days, I lived off nothing. Luckily, I convinced the owner of my accommodation to let me stay free of charge, provided I paid when my friend arrived.

DIY Marketing

When I came back from Ecuador, I was ready to go. I did a bit of bartending and waitering on the side and started producing my black and white photocopied marketing materials. I blanketed the university campuses and set up speaking arrangements wherever anyone would listen to me. The people at Mountain Equipment Co-op gave me a platform in their downtown Toronto store. They would make in-store announcements like, "For the next hour, if you buy one life jacket, you get the second one free. And, in the canoe department, Bruce Poon Tip will be speaking about adventure tourism."

The more people I spoke to, the more I knew I was tapping into something real. All I needed to do was sign people up and ensure that everything went according to plan. I kept writing long letters to tribesmen (this was pre-email, when even faxes were still new), outlining what the trip would require resource-wise. In the end, I managed to book six people and the trip went off without a hitch. The crowd weren't backpackers at all, but thirty-something professionals who were looking for something other than the status quo travel experience.

The success of the first trip made things easier. G.A.P suddenly had some word of mouth. But I was still working other jobs and avoiding my landlord. The second trip was to Belize. I advertised that we would be canoeing along the Macaw River. After driving the canoes down from Los Angeles, however, the travellers and operators were stopped and detained by local authorities. The Belizean government didn't want tourists traipsing around the interior. They wanted everyone to stick to the beaches. Besides, they had never encountered canoes before and they weren't at all convinced they were safe. Luckily for us, Belize is a small country and the minister of tourism's office was down the street from a hotel we were staying at. Eventually, I was able to convince him to allow us to use canoes, provided the boats were steered by locals. In the end, the whole incident added a certain sense of adventure to the tour. Nobody left feeling cheated.

Overcoming a Serious Hurdle

After two years of running the business, it occurred to me that G.A.P would never be able to seriously grow so long as we were tied to the North American market. Canadians and Americans only get an average of two weeks of holiday per year. I never thought Europeans or Australians got any more than we did, but the second I found out, it became strikingly clear G.A.P needed to tap those markets. The problem was how. It was unheard of for a German tourist to buy his travel package from a Canadian company. The more I thought about it, the more I questioned why that had to be true. Why couldn't the wall come down? Why couldn't the industry open up?

It wasn't easy by any stretch of the imagination, but I flew over to Europe for trade shows, met people, made connections, and tried to sell them on my passion and the quality of the G.A.P idea. I didn't fit in at all. The tourism industry in Europe was (and still is) a very stodgy one. I was a kid, a Canadian who spoke neither French nor German, and a visible minority. Who did I think I was? Luckily, it helped that there were no companies in Europe doing what I was doing, so at the very least, I benefited from being novel. In the end, the passion won enough people over and G.A.P slowly began to attain an international reach. Today, 80 percent of our business is international. If I hadn't succeeded on my European trips, who knows where we would be now?

Surviving in Isolation

Starting a business looks romantic from a distance, but the period when I was getting G.A.P off the ground was a very isolating one. That's not to say it wasn't remarkably fun. I was having the time of my life. But I lost touch with a lot of people. Old friends couldn't understand why I always needed to be working or why I wasn't hitting the social scene. Other friends were moving on to have families and settle down. I wasn't at the same stage of life as they were. I was in no rush to do those things — my entire life was devoted to the business. I needed to scrimp, save, and hustle. As a result, I didn't have the amount of support I might have liked.

Luckily, as the company came to be better known, I started meeting more people like myself: people who had sacrificed everything for a vision; people who understood what I had gone through because they had gone through it as well. In a way, I found a new community in the end. But if you are going to be successful with a business, you need to be prepared to survive in that isolation.